Something old . . .
something new . . .
something borrowed

Bride's-eye View of Cooking Cookbook

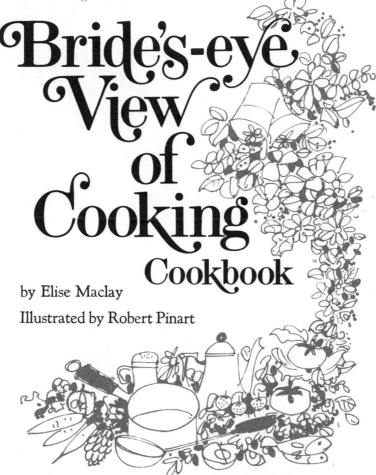

by Elise Maclay

Illustrated by Robert Pinart

Published by The C. R. Gibson Company, Norwalk, Connecticut

Confidentially

    This book was going to have a subtitle but it was too long to fit on the cover. I was going to add that it will tell you everything you never wanted to know about cooking before but want to know now.

    Like how do you do it every night? After all, when you were single and invited a man for an intimate little dinner at your place on a Friday night, you had all week to plan the menu, a paycheck to blow on filet mignon and artichokes, Wednesday night to market, Thursday night to scrub mushrooms and Friday morning to set the table and chill the wine. What happens when the man becomes a husband and comes home for one of your intimate little dinners every night?

    You can't demolish a paycheck to buy gourmet foods without demolishing your image as a thrifty helpmeet. You can't be scrubbing mushrooms for Friday night's dinner on Thursday night because on Thursday night you'll be cooking Thursday night's dinner which you can't have got ready on Wednesday night because on Wednesday night you were cooking Wednesday night's dinner and how did you ever get into this and how do you get out and how come all those pretty cookbooks you've collected aren't any help? I'll tell you why. Because they're full of recipes. That's why.

    Now I have nothing against recipes. In fact, I'm crazy about them. I have boxes, baskets, envelopes and file cabinets full of them. My favorites are in this book. But recipes are most useful after you've done a lot of cooking. But in the beginning, while you're still shaking rice out of your veil, you need to know a lot of other things. Like what utensils to use. What staples to have on the shelf. How much of everything to buy. How to work and cook. How to impress old friends, new friends and inlaws. How to plan menus that are pennywise, posh and possible. (Steak Diane, whipped potatoes and zabaglione are not possible because they're all two-handed dishes you do at the last minute and nobody has that many hands or last minutes.) You should also know how to carve what you cook and present it prettily. Don't expect your platters to look like the magazine pictures, though. Because, frankly, they cheat. I once saw a food stylist (yes, Virginia, in the wild and wacky world of advertising there are such things) varnish a turkey. They also tend to garnish more lavishly than any food budget I've been on will allow.

Watercress, water chestnuts, mushroom caps filled with caviar, baby beets filled with sour cream, filberts foamed in butter are eye-catching on a four-color page, and no doubt marvelous to munch, but like the extras on a new car, they do up the cost. Happily, there are ways to present food dramatically without doing violence to your budget. A centerpiece of shells for a seafood dinner. Steak en planque, using your breadboard. Sherbet in champagne glasses. Anything in a basket. Parsley and chives, easy to grow on a windowsill and deliciously decorative scissor-snipped into or onto everything.

So hang onto all those cookbooks you've collected, and collect more. But begin at the beginning. With a bride's-eye view.

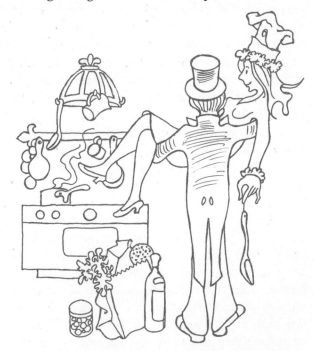

Contents

Something Old

Something New

Something Borrowed

Bride's-Eye View

THE PENNYWISE BRIDE

THE NATURAL BRIDE

THE ENTERTAINING BRIDE

THE OUTDOOR BRIDE

THE SENSUOUS BRIDE

THE DISAPPEARING BRIDE

BUYING GUIDES

Something Old

YOU LEARNED IT ALL ONCE

You learned it all in school, once. Weights and measures. How many teaspoons in a tablespoon. How many cups in a pint or a quart or a pound. But you've forgotten a lot of it and you're feeling a little uneasy. Now that you're about to be a Serious Cook, shouldn't you know all this?

No. That's what cookbooks are for. Most of them, this one included, have lists and tables. But you won't use them all that often. Because few recipes call for a pint or a pound. They *tell* you how many cups. That is, they tell you how many cups to use — not how much to buy. You need to know, of course. For how much of what to buy, see page 112.

But what do you buy? The makings of meals your man will be mad about. What foods do American men like best? A leading magazine recently asked. Here are the answers in the order of their popularity.

MEN'S FAVORITE FOODS

1. Broiled steak
2. Roast beef
3. Fried chicken
4. Baked ham
5. Braised Pork Chops
6. Spaghetti with meat sauce
7. Apple Pie
8. Strawberry Shortcake
9. Ice cream
10. Broiled hamburgers
11. Beef Stew
12. Baked beans

Of course, your man may favor pizza or Kentucky Fried Chicken, in which case you probably don't need this book. Or he may be a true gourmet, opting for Coq au Vin — don't despair, we know a quick, easy way to make that, too. The recipe's on page 67.

However, for the most part, you'll notice that the foods which are top favorites with men tend to be familiar, un-exotic, basic. Because they are so familiar, un-fancy and old-timey, these are the foods which most men assume any and every woman in the whole wide world — and certainly brilliant little you — can prepare at the drop of a suggestion, eyes-shut and with one hand tied behind your back. If you can, skip the rest of this chapter and browse about in chapter 2, while the rest of us bone up on what our husbands blithely assume we already know.

POTS AND PANS

What about what to cook it in? I've seen lists of have-to-haves a mile long. Cooking utensils are pretty and fun to collect but it's amazing how many you can do without. I'm not suggesting that you do, but never let the fact that you haven't a hundred beautiful pots and pans keep you from cooking a hundred beautiful things to eat. As for bare essentials, all you really need are: flat things — skillets — one large, one small. And deep things — saucepans — one large, one small. All with covers. As heavy as possible. To bake, you'll need two pie pans and two cake tins and a cookie sheet, but these can be of foil. In addition, you'll want a Dutch oven which isn't an oven at all but a heavy iron pot, enamelled, perhaps, with a tight fitting cover, which can sit atop the stove or go into the oven. At least one casserole to begin with — add others when you find out whether or not he likes casserole dishes. If you get skillets with oven-proof handles, or wood handles which detach, you can bake things like scallopini and fish fillets in a skillet in the oven.

We're still not ready for recipes. Because recipes say things like "sprinkle with garlic salt". Do you have garlic salt among your staples? What staples? Turn to page 116 for a concise bride's-eye view.

How does anyone manage to have all these on hand at once? They don't. And if you're wise, you won't even try to pay for it all at once. Instead, you'll buy the basics and add a small can of this or that each time you market. Stash away your treasures on a top shelf and wait for emergency to strike. When great-aunt Agatha arrives unexpectedly, you'll be glad you went all out for crab meat. If she never comes, you can invent an occasion and dine deluxe with the husband of your choice.

HOW TO COMPOSE A MENU

For guidelines, all you really need to remember is: Contrast. In color, texture and taste. Cauliflower, whipped potatoes and Veal in Cream are not going to do much to delight the eye. If you choose a more exciting color combination — Veal in Cream, tossed greens, bran muffins and grilled tomato — you come out beautifully in the vitamin department, too. I sometimes get the feeling that Mother Nature subsidizes culinary art. Because foods of different colors have different nutritional values. Put a green, leafy thing next to a red or orange root thing, add fish, fowl or meat, and you've got a more or less balanced meal as well as a pretty color combination.

Textural contrasts are what make you a sensual cook. Consider a classic: a mealy Idaho potato, topped with the velvety smoothness of sour cream, topped with crunchy bacon bits. Contemplate the simple delight of crisp cookies with ice cream, scrambled eggs with super-crisp bacon, croutons afloat in a bowl of cream soup. Or more exotic textural contrasts: water chestnuts in the Chicken à la King, toasted, slivered almonds strewn over filet of sole. Happily, lots of foods you're likely to think of serving together do differ in texture. If not, a single substitution will often do the trick — shoestring potatoes instead of mashed, raw celery instead of creamed. Or you can simply add the missing texture — the aforementioned bacon bits, toasted almonds and croutons being cases in point. A tiny bit of trouble, but guaranteed to win friends and influence husbands.

As for contrasts in taste, these happen to happen more often than not. I mean you wouldn't serve a meal consisting of everything spicy or everything sweet or everything salty or everything bland, would you? I thought not.

Since a meal should probably not consist of apple pie, alone, we'll take up each food preference in a total-meal context. Beginning with (number 1) Broiled Steak Dinner. But since this is, after all, a bride's-eye view, it can't be just a steak dinner. Ours is to be a Super-Sirloin Marchand du Vin. With spinach salad, and strawberry shortcake. We've chosen this menu not only because it's balanced and beautiful, festive and fun, elegant and exciting, but also because it's possible. Steak-and-baked-potato are fine for a restaurant, but most home ovens don't bake and broil at the same time. And while there are ways to crisp frozen french fries on top of the stove, the way it works out is that you have to watch them and then you're likely to forget to watch the steak for doneness which, aside from buying a good piece of meat to begin with, is the whole secret of sirloin success.

15

Super Sirloin Steak au Marchand de Vin

Buy a good piece of sirloin, which in practice means buy it from a market or butcher you can trust. If possible, have it at room temperature. Slash the fat around the edges. This will keep the steak from curling. Preheat the broiler. Put the broiler pan with rack two inches from the heat. Broil on one side, turn with tongs (if you stick it with a fork, the juice will run out) and broil on the other side. Don't forget to set your oven regulator at "broil". I know that's pretty obvious, but I still sometimes forget. And close the door if it's a gas range, leave the door ajar if it's electric. Here's the doneness countdown:

Minutes per lb. for 1 inch thick steak

Rare: 5 minutes on each side

Medium: 6 minutes on each side

Well-done: 8 minutes on each side

Serve immediately on a hot platter with *Marchand de Vin Sauce*, which couldn't be easier to make. Heat *canned brown gravy* with an equal amount of *red wine*.

Spinach Salad

Wash and dry *1 pound (or one package) fresh spinach.* Cut *2 slices bacon* into 1 inch pieces and place in pan, cook until crisp. Add *¼ cup vinegar, ½ cup olive oil, Worcestershire sauce* and *salt and pepper* to taste. Then pour the dressing over the spinach and mix thoroughly. Pour while it's still hot because the whole point is to wilt the spinach and make it mouth-wateringly tender.

Strawberry Shortcake

Before you start your steak — or in the morning — squeeze the *juice 1 orange* over *fresh strawberries.* Stir in a tablespoon or two of *brown sugar.* If you have time, make *biscuits* from a mix. If not, buy bakery biscuits and put them in the oven to utilize the heat left over after broiling your steak. At dessert time, spoon berries over biscuits and top with clouds of *sweetened whipped cream.*

Finale: instant espresso

That's for Friday night. But we promised to tell you how to do it *every* night. While that's not quite as easy as A.B.C., it is as easy as M.M.M. Menu. Market. Make it.

17

FOOD MARKETING

Now that you know how to plan a menu, plan seven, one for every day of the week, go to the market and buy everything you need. If you succeed, run for president. Nobody I know manages not to come home without bread, beer, salt or sesame seeds. I tend to forget whole categories — vegetables, meat — which makes it a lot harder to make-do-without, and is a good argument for marketing on Thursday night. The stores are less crowded then, the weekend specials are on, and you have Friday night and Sat-urday to fill in the blanks.

Now you may have a husband who likes to do the marketing with you or by himself. I'd be a bit dubious about the latter in-clination. The check-out girl may be better stacked than the shelves. However, shopping together can be very companionable. Also many men need to be educated as to how much food-in-the-raw, as opposed to restaurant food, actually costs, and watching the tariff mount on a wire basket full of comestibles is certainly educational. A word of warning. At least in grocery stores, men tend to do a lot more impulse buying than women do. And while things like smoked oysters and marrons glacé are nice to have on hand, it's hard to compose a meal of them, which, unless your food budget is more elastic than most, is what you're likely to end up trying to do.

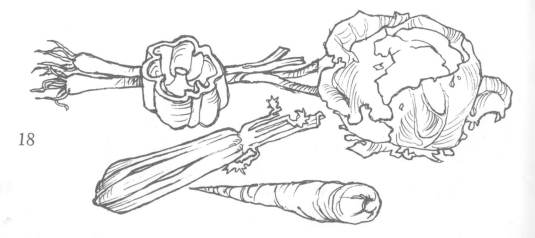

As for money-saving marketing, head for the nearest honest-to-goodness, genuine supermarket. One with name-brand equivalents and unit pricing. Read. Comparison shop. And go slow on quantity buying. For brides it's often a mixed blessing. How many times a day do you want to eat fresh peaches? Have you the equipment, time and energy to can them? Will you really bake three peach pies and if you do is there room in your freezer to store them? Many "2-for" bargains involve a saving of only a penny, so if the extra loaf of bread or box of tea is likely to hang around the house until it's stale, spend the extra penny and buy only one.

THURSDAY NIGHT THINGS

Now that I've talked you into doing your marketing on Thursday nights, I feel it's only fair to let you in on some of my super-secret, super-swift Thursday Night Things. After all, supermarkets close at nine. So you'll have to be quick-be-nimble with a skillet before you go or, after you get back, manage to concoct something marvelous with your right hand while you're putting the produce away with your left.

Home economists opt for eating before you go. You'll buy less, spend less money because nothing will look very appealing to you. A dreary idea if I ever heard one. My way is to go food shopping when you're ravenous. Then, when you hit the supermarket, you'll feel like a kid in a toystore. With money to spend. Hang onto your market list and you're safe to have fun. And picking out a beautiful bunch of grapes, a juicy roast, a jar of strawberry jam *is* a privilege and a delight.

But when you bring your bulging brown bags home and start stashing your newly acquired goodies away, you are not going to feel like cooking up a storm. You won't have to, if sitting on the second shelf of your refrigerator is a Thursday Night Thing.

Sorta-Souffle   19

You make this the night before or in the morning. It will take less than 5 minutes. In the evening, when you return from marketing, the first thing you do is turn the oven on, to 350°. Next, put the frozen foods away. Now take the Thursday Thing from the refrigerator and put it in the oven. By the time you've put the rest of the groceries away, and slipped into something your husband likes to see you in, your Sorta-Souffle will be ready. Serve it with crisp cold apples or sliced tomatoes.

To make this marvel, you'll need: *1 egg, 1 cup milk, ½ pound grated cheese, 6 slices bread,* buttered, crusts removed. You can use sharp, yellow cheese, Gruyere, which you can't exactly grate but you can snip into tiny pieces with a scissors or Swiss cheese. Put two pieces of the buttered bread in the bottom of a small (1 quart) casserole or baking dish. Put some of the cheese on top. Put two more slices of buttered bread on top of that, more cheese on top of that. Cover with your last two slices of buttered bread. Beat the egg and milk together and pour around the sides of the casserole first, then on top. Into the refrigerator now until you come home from market. If it's not marketing day, let this Sorta-Souffle stand at least four hours. Bake it about 30 minutes.

As it bakes, it will puff up all fluffy and golden and it needn't be served "at once" as honest-to-goodness souffles demand. Altogether a very satisfactory Thursday Night Thing.

Luxe Soup

Another good Thursday Night Thing is a bowl of soup so rich and creamy, so heady and elegant it would be unthinkable to serve anything at all with it — except, perhaps, after a decent interval, lemon or lime sherbet and a thimbleful of black coffee. Such a soup can be made in minutes.

Pour *1 jigger sherry* over a *medium-sized can lobster*. Let it stand while you combine *1 can condensed pea soup* with *½ can condensed tomato soup* and *1 cup cream*. Bring the mixture to a boil. Add the lobster and sherry, heat thoroughly. Just before serving, add an extra tablespoon of sherry.

Thursday Night Salad Thing

It does seem to me that the younger a man is, the more likely he is to like salad. A real, robust, man-pleasing salad. And it's made this way. With clean, crisp, dry greens. Lettuce, Escarole. Spinach. Watercress. Any or all. Plus vegetables — whatever you happen to have left-over. Tomatoes. Onions. Cucumbers. If you have half a cup of cooked peas or a boiled potato, toss them in. Cube the potato first, of course, or slice it. At this point most cookbooks will adjure you to add "matchstick slices of meat and cheese." But put down that knife. Some day women's liberationists may arrange it so that boys and girls are brought up in exactly the same way. Until then, most of us females are sure to feel a lot more comfortable with a pair of scissors than with a knife. Therefore, not just for making this salad but forevermore, supply yourself with a pair of sturdy scissors, keep them in the kitchen, and let them never depart. You'll use them in dozens of ways, about which we'll talk later. Now we're talking about adding meat and cheese.

Traditionally, a chef's salad contains matchstick slices of cooked chicken, ham, tongue and Swiss Cheese. I don't know about you, but I never have cooked chicken on hand to slice into a salad. A slice or two of boiled ham which didn't get into the weekend sandwiches, yes. A scrap of cold roast beef. Genoa Salami. That's the sort of thing I find in my refrigerator of a Thursday night. Happily, snipped into strips with a scissor, any or all of these

make perky salad additions. Swiss, as we have said, is traditional. But a snappy yellow cheese is good, too. If the cheese you choose is too soft to cut well, simply crumble it into the salad.

If what you've compiled so far looks hearty and hefty, cease and desist. If it looks a bit skimpy and you're starved, add a can of anchovies, oil and all, or a can of tuna.

The prettiest way to arrange all this is with the greens on the bottom of a big salad bowl, vegetables next, meat and cheese on top. Pour over all 1 cup of French dressing. Not from the market. Your own. Easiest thing in the world to make. Just put *⅔ cup olive oil* in a mason jar, add *⅓ cup wine vinegar* and a dash of *salt and pepper*. Shake. Pour. Toss.

22

For full effect, do the pouring and tossing at the table. Serve on chilled plates — an impressive touch, achieved with virtually no effort — merely aforethought to put two plates in the refrigerator before you dash off to work or wherever in the morning. As they keep telling us, it's the little things (diamonds?) that count.

SATURDAY THINGS

While Thursday Things should be quick to compile and cook and should involve as few ingredients, utensils, pots and pans as possible, Saturday Things are something else. If you're ever going to do any serious cooking, Saturday's the time to do it. Not only because there probably isn't any other time to, but also because there's something soul satisfying about filling the house with the fragrance of bread baking. It's somehow merry to have a stewpot bubbling and burbling on the back of the stove. And it definitely adds an air of importance to the day to have a noble roast or a fine fat bird browning in the oven, to be looked at and perhaps basted (that means spooning some juice over it) now and again.

*   *   *

Bread? By a bride? Definitely. Because bread is one of the easiest things in the world to make. Forget all those jokes about the bride's biscuits being hard as rock and heavy as lead because biscuits are a lot harder than bread is to make. If you treat biscuit dough rough it gets tough. Not so bread dough. In fact when you beat

23

and batter bread dough, it's called kneading and the finished loaf responds by rising to new heights.

Doesn't bread take hours to make? No. *Making* bread takes about 25 minutes. *Baking* it takes 55. The rest of the time — about three hours — you just go your way while the bread is doing its own thing: rising.

You can, of course, make bread from a hot roll mix. You can even, with imagination, herbs and spices, do fantastic things to store-bought breadstuffs. More about that later. What we're into here is what to do when your mouth is watering for some real old fashioned home-made bread, and you feel like being the warm, earth-mothery goddess who creates it.

It is quite possible to make bread from only five ingredients: water, yeast, shortening, salt and flour. But you only save ingredients, not time and energy. Frankly, when I take the time and trouble to make bread, I don't want to end up with an ordinary loaf. I want something downright voluptuous, bursting with goodness, with an aroma that drives men wild. I want thick slices of it slathered with butter. I want everyone who tastes it to swoon. In short, the only bread worth baking is a no-holds-barred, all-the-stops-out, ultra-everything bread like this:

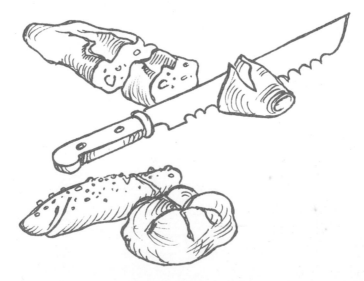

24

Note: I go to the local bakery and get 20¢ worth of fresh yeast. What with the changing price of everything, better ask for enough to make 4 loaves.

Put *5½ cups milk* into a saucepan and bring to a boil. Remove from heat and add 3 *tablespoons butter, 5½ teaspoons salt* and *5½ tablespoons sugar*. Set aside to become lukewarm.

Pour *⅔ cup lukewarm water* into a bowl, add *2 teaspoons sugar*, add *yeast,* and stir until dissolved. Set this aside.

Sift *16 cups flour* into a large container.

To mix the batter, it's nice to have a large crockery bowl. Pour the milk mixture in to the bowl and gradually add 4 or 5 cups of flour, stirring regularly to make a good batter. Then pour the yeast mixture in and stir well. Add most of the remaining flour until the batter is very stiff. Turn this out on a floured board and knead thoroughly for about 5 minutes — sometimes a little longer. Wash the crockery bowl and grease it lightly. Put dough in the bowl, turning it over so that a light covering of *butter,* Crisco or whatever covers the mass. (The whatever could be salad oil). The next step is to let the dough rise in a place where the temperature is between 80° and 85°. One way to do this is to put it in an oven that has been only slightly warmed. It is important not to have the temperature more than 85°. A hand in the oven will tell you whether it is too hot. Cover the bowl with a damp cloth and leave it for about $1\frac{1}{2}$ hours, by which time the dough should have doubled in size. Take it out and push it down thoroughly, folding the edges in towards the center. Turn it over, cover with a damp cloth and let it rise again for about 30 minutes, during which it will again double in size.

Now turn it out on a board and, with a knife, cut it in two, then into 4 pieces. Shape each piece into a smooth ball and cover the 4 balls with a damp towel and let rise for about 10 minutes while you grease four breadpans. Take one of the balls and flatten it out on the board into an oblong shape. Fold it in half lengthwise and then pick up the dough by the ends and pull it apart, slapping the board several times until the dough measures about

15″ by 5″ by 1″. Then bring the two ends to the center, over-lapping them. Fold in two sides towards the center, sealing them with your hand, so that the dough is now about the shape of the breadpan. Roll it back and forth a bit to tighten it. Do the same with the remaining 3 balls and put each one in a loaf pan and cover them with a damp towel. Put them in the same slightly warm oven and let them rise for about an hour, during which they will double in size. Take them out. Preheat the oven to 360.° Put the breadpans back in the oven and bake for 55 minutes. Turn the loaves out on cooling racks. Enjoy.

While most fruit breads and nut breads can be made from a mix, and if so, why not, I think you should know how to make Banana Bread. Because sooner or later in your married life you are going to find yourself with three bananas which are getting too ripe. Besides, this Banana Bread is so good it's worth going out and buying bananas so you can make it. It's a nice friendly recipe, too, because you don't even beat the eggs, much less separate them. And you just throw in the dry ingredients without sifting them together — or at all.

Banana Bread

Crush 3 *bananas* and whip with eggbeater till very light. Cream together (that means mash around with a big tablespoon) *½ cup margarine* and *1 cup sugar*. Stir in *two eggs, 2 cups flour; 1 tea-spoon baking soda, ½ teaspoon salt, ¼ cup nut meats*. Add the whipped bananas. Bake in a greased pan 1 hour at 350°.

Two Easy Ways To Do Chicken

The easiest thing in the world to do to a chicken is to *salt* and *pepper* a whole *broiling chicken* and bake it in a 350° oven for forty minutes. You don't *have* to do a thing to it but look in and gloat as it gets brown. You can sprinkle white wine over it every so often, or spoon up some of the fat that runs out and douse that over the top, but honestly, you don't have to. Today's broiling and frying chickens are tender and plump and completely self-sufficient in the oven.

A little more trouble and even more impressive chicken is to stuff a small *whole chicken* with a *packaged mix*. Again, once you've popped your bird in the oven, go your way, win at Mah-Jongg or plant tulips. I don't care what Grandma's old cookbook says, you don't have to baste.

Do-Nothing Leg of Lamb

Another no-baste Saturday Thing is roast leg of lamb. Choose a *2 to 2½ pound roast*. Heat oven to 325°. Season meat with *salt* and *pepper*. Place fat side up on a rack in an open pan. Roast meat. Do not baste. Do not cover. Do not add water. I like lamb rare — ½ hour of roasting per pound. If you like yours well-done, roast for 1 hour per lb. Serve surrounded by canned pear halves filled with mint jelly.

27

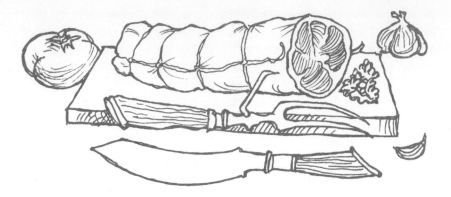

Do-Nothing Roast Beef

Since men list this as their second favorite dish, it certainly is nice that it's so easy. A beautiful Saturday thing. Again the procedure is to salt and pepper the meat, place fat side up on a rack in an open shallow roasting pan. Do not baste. Do not cover. Do not add water. At 300° your roast will be:

Rare if you cook it 18 minutes per pound.

Medium if you cook it 22 minutes per pound.

Well-done if you cook it 30 minutes per pound.

Saturday Stew

But about that burbling on the back of the stove. Most men enter sniffing and hope that it's stew. Everybody and his brother has a favorite stew recipe. The problem with most of them is that they call for too many ingredients. I once saw a recipe that required 24 different ingredients — including fresh lemon juice, and grated rind. Somehow when I'm in a stew mood, I'm not thinking of fresh lemons. I am thinking of rich brown gravy and succulent chunks of beef taking care of itself on the stove while I work my macrame. As far as ingredients go, you can go as far as you like. Potatoes. Carrots. Leeks. Peas. Turnips. Add what you will. Or add none of them and at the last minute whip up some Minute Rice to spoon this succulent stew over. Whatever you do, reserve about 3 hours for this Saturday Stew to burble.

In a heavy frying pan, saute *2 onions,* sliced paper thin. Bacon fat is the best fat to use for this. You do save yours, don't you? If not, start now. Now take the onions out of the pan and save them. Toss in *2 pounds stew meat.* It comes in cubes. Brown the meat on all sides. Take your time, and get them really brown. Sprinkle them with *flour* (a tablespoon will do) and *salt* and *pepper.* If you have it, add a pinch of marjoram or thyme. Dump all this into a big flame-proof casserole or stew pot with a lid. Pour *1 cup beef broth* (or *1 bouillon cube* dissolved in water) into the frying pan. Scrape around — preferably with a wooden spoon — to get all the brown bits up. Pour into the casserole. Now add *1 cup dry red wine.* Cover the pot and let it cook very slowly for three hours. Look at it now and again and if it seems to be getting too thick, add water, broth or wine. I'd opt for wine. After three hours add the onions you've browned and saved along with as many *fresh mushrooms* as you can afford. Stir, cover, and let cook very slowly until you're ready to eat. Just before serving stir in a couple of tablespoons of brandy.

While these Saturday Things are fine company fare, I suggest that you sometimes make them on a Saturday when nobody's coming. Because it's a glorious feeling to wake up on Sunday knowing there's cold roast chicken, or lamb or lean roast beef in the refrigerator. Most cookbooks will tell you lots of dishes you can concoct out of cold roast chicken, lamb or roast beef, but frankly, I wouldn't make any of them because cold roast chicken, lamb and roast beef are too good to tamper with. As for left-over stew, you just heat it up and discover it tastes better than it did the day before.

Speaking of company, however, you may want to do something a little more dazzling. So let's move on to some Company's Coming Saturday Specials.

COMPANY FARE

Filet of Sole With Shrimp

Buy enough *sole* for each person to have one piece. Buy enough *cooked shrimp* for each person to have five. Place sole in a buttered

baking dish, *salt* and *pepper* the sole and place shrimp on top. Make a sauce by adding *½ can cream* to *1 can cream of chicken soup*. Mix in *1 tablespoon capers*. Pour this sauce over the shrimp and sole. Cover and bake at 350° for 30 minutes. Serve with baked tomato halves, green rice (made by adding chopped parsley to cooked rice), and lemon ice, for dessert.

Artichicken

This is an easy, impressive dish. There are lot of versions, but I like this one best.

Turn the oven to 350°. In a heavy skillet, brown a 3 *pound cut-up fryer* in *butter*. Remove to a casserole. Pour *¼ cup brandy*

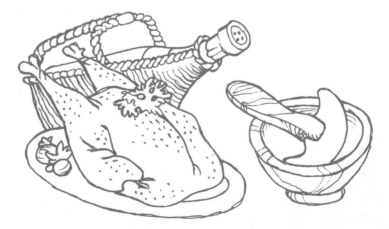

over the chicken and touch a match to it. It will flame up beautifully and smell delicious. When the flame dies out, add *2 cups dry
white wine, salt, pepper,* and *1 teaspoon rosemary.* Cover and bake
40 minutes. Add one *15 ½-ounce can of artichoke hearts* — plain,
not packed in oil. Bake an additional 10 minutes.

Saturday Chops

Pork should always, always be thoroughly cooked. Which more
or less relegates it to Saturday. If you're going to refinish furni-

ture or go for a hike, here's a dish you can put together in the
morning, refrigerate, and pop into the oven while you're getting
the turpentine off your hands or doffing your hiking gear. Begin
by pouring boiling water over *½ cup raisins.* This will turn them
from hard, wrinkly things to plump juicy things. Brown a couple
of nice *thick pork chops* in *butter* or margarine. *Salt* and *pepper*
them and place them in a covered baking dish. Peel, core and slice
a *big apple* and strew the slices over the chops. Drain the raisins
and add them. Add *½ cup broth* (which can be a bouillon cube
dissolved in water) or *½ cup cider.* Sprinkle with *1 tablespoon
brown sugar* and the merest smidgen — less than *¼ teaspoon dry
mustard* and *powdered cloves.* Refrigerate. Do your own thing.

Towards twilight, bake covered in a 375° oven for one hour. Uncover and bake 15 minutes longer. Peek at it now and again during the baking and add more liquid if things start looking too dry. Serve with rice and something green.

Quick-Stuff Chops

These look like a big deal, are hearty and filling, and extra-easy. Supply yourself with a package of *poultry stuffing* and *two double-thick pork chops*. Ask the butcher to cut a pocket in the chops. Make up a cup of stuffing according to directions on the package. Save the rest in an airtight container. Fill the pockets in the chops with the stuffing. Skewer the edges together or tie with string. Sprinkle with *salt* and *pepper*. Place in an uncovered roasting pan and bake for 20 minutes at 400°. The purpose of this maneuver is to avoid having to brown the chops in a skillet first — a spattery business and you have to stand there and watch. After twenty minutes, reduce oven heat to 300°, add *1 cup water or dry white wine,* cover and bake for one hour. Again it does no harm to look in on things from time to time and add more liquid if necessary.

On account of the stuffing, you won't need rice or noodles or potatoes with this. Just something like broccoli and a salad made from icy slices of orange, onion rings and lettuce with a dribble of oil and vinegar. Dessert suggestion: Gingersnaps spread with cream cheese.

Pot Roast Undressed

If you have a husband who hankers for pot roast the way his mother makes it, get his mother's recipe. Because everybody and his mother seems to have a different idea as to the best way for a roast to go to pot. There are Italian versions with tomato sauce, German versions with crumbled ginger snaps and French versions with wine. Some marry the meat to carrots and leeks, potatoes and onions. Some swear by the addition of celery. In short, you can dress up a pot roast any number of ways. But as a bride, you might begin with pot roast undressed.

Buy a pot roast. Look for rump roast or beef chuck pot roast or bottom round. Be sure it's in one piece — not several tied to-

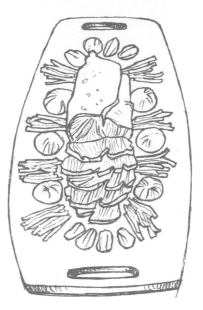

gether. You can usually see, but if you're not sure, ask. The trouble with composite roasts is they won't slice nicely and you want cold pot roast slices for sandwiches, don't you?

Put the pot roast in a heavy iron Dutch oven or enameled steel casserole with a tight lid. Put this pot on the stove and turn the heat up high. Brown the meat on all sides. There will probably be plenty of fat on the meat, but if it's altogether lean on one side, begin with the fat side down. Turn till the meat is really brown on all sides. Don't hurry and don't worry about the smoke. You're *cooking*. Now turn the heat as low as possible and let the pot roast pot. Be sure the lid is on tight. At the end of 3 hours, lift the lid and add *salt* and *pepper*. If you like thin gravy, you've got it. If you prefer thick gravy, muddle a little butter and flour together in a teacup and add this, a spoonful at a time, to the gravy, stirring hard.

If your man's a meat-and-potatoes man, interrupt your pot roast after two hours and add three or four small potatoes — peeled or unpeeled, depending upon how healthy you want to be and how ambitious you feel. Replace lid and cook an hour more, turning the potatoes every so often to brown them on all sides.

SWEET AND SLOW DESSERTS

As long as you have bread rising and stew simmering, you might as well have something good going for dessert. The loveliest, laziest, longest-cooking dessert I know is *Flim Flan*. I'll tell you how to make it if you promise to serve it in crystal champagne glasses, paper-thin rice bowls or your best teacups. Presentation is part of it. And while making it, send your man off to adjust the hi-fi because a little mystery is good for any marriage and he might as well marvel at how you could have whipped up such a fabulous dessert while you spent the afternoon holding up the shelf he was installing. I guarantee he'll never guess. If he peeks, he'll think you're off your rocker because this is what you do.

Flim Flan

Put an unopened can of *sweetened condensed milk* in a saucepan of water. Be sure the water completely covers the can. Simmer for three hours. Yes, honestly. Be sure the water doesn't boil away. After three hours, pour off the hot water, cool the can under cold water, and put it in the refrigerator until you're ready to serve. At serving time, open the can and spoon out smooth, creamy, dark caramelized custard into those pretty glasses or bowls you promised you'd use.

Real Thing Apple Pie

If your man doesn't need you to hold up one end of a shelf, and you feel like doing something deliciously domestic, it's definitely time to bake an apple pie. There are, I'm sure you know, pie crust mixes, pastry sticks, and frozen unbaked pie shells you simply fill with a can of apple pie mix and bake. Good they all are. But Saturday's the day for more soul-satisfying pursuits.

So you can say, I did it myself. So you can feel like a pioneer lady in a sunbonnet. And so if you find yourself somewhere where there are no convenience foods, you'll know how.

For the crust: Put *1⅓ cups all-purpose flour* (not cake flour) in a bowl with *½ cup shortening* and *¼ teaspoon salt*. If you got a pastry blender as a shower gift, use it. If not, use two knives. Cut the shortening into the flour until it looks like coarse corn meal. Add, a little at a time, *three or four tablespoons ice-cold water,* blending in as quickly as possible. Take half the moistened flour and roll it into a ball. Place between two sheets of waxed paper and roll it out with that rolling pin they keep making jokes about. If you haven't a rolling pin, you can use a bottle, but it's hard to do as neat a job. Roll from the center out. When you have a nice pie-pan size sheet, fold it in half — lightly, don't crease — and transfer it to a greased, pie plate or tin. The folding is to make it easy to pick up. You'll do the same with the second portion of dough which will serve as the top crust.

For filling: Peel and slice thin enough *apples to make 5 cups.* Mix with *¾ cup sugar, ¾ teaspoon cinnamon, ¼ teaspoon nutmeg.*

Heap filling in pastry-lined pie pan. Dot with butter. Cover with top crust. Cut two or three slits in the top crust to let the

steam escape. Seal edges with pastry crimper or fork. Bake in 425° oven 50 to 60 minutes until crust is browned and apples are cooked.

Serve warm with ice cream or sharp cheddar cheese.

Old Fashioned Devil's Food Cake

There are lots of chocolate cake mixes on the market. They're good. But somehow, they don't taste quite the same, they don't send out quite the heady aroma, in short, they're just not as devil-ishly good as the devil's food cake my mother used to make. My mother still makes devil's food cake, but she uses a mix, now. Convenience corrupts. But you're still pure in heart and possessed of gilt-edged intentions and a hungry devil of a husband. So I be-queath my mother's devil's food recipe to you.

Combine, melt and set aside: *3 squares bitter chocolate, ¼ pound butter, ½ cup double strength coffee (½ teaspoon instant coffee with ½ cup water).*

Sift together: *2 cups sifted cake flour, 1½ teaspoons baking soda, ½ teaspoon salt.*

Mix together: *1½ cups sugar, ½ pint sour cream, 2½ tea-spoons vanilla.*

Add *2 eggs* well beaten. Mix in ⅓ of the chocolate mixture, then ⅓ of the dry ingredients. Repeat, beating thoroughly as you go. Bake in two greased 8-inch cake pans at 350° for 35 minutes.

Something New

FROZEN FANCIES AND MARVELOUS MIXES

People who say there's nothing new under the sun don't shop in supermarkets. Every day new products appear, new mixes materialize, frozen fancies proliferate. Everything keeps coming in new flavors and forms. A jaded friend of mine was advised by her psychiatrist to cook something different each day. Being lazy as well as jaded, she decided to stick to mixes and convenience foods. That was two years ago. She's still cooking something different every day and she hasn't got past aisle "C".

There's only one thing wrong with having so much to choose from. It's hard to choose. Noodles with cheese sauce, chicken sauce, sour cream sauce, Romanoff and Italian style are all available and good. And there are so many variations on the instant rice theme.

Don't let it throw you. Work from right to left. Or close your eyes and reach. If you're tempted to deliberate too long, remember the story about the man who reluctantly hired an eighty-year-old farm hand. The first day the old codger pitched hay from dawn till dusk. The second day he did the same. The third day he again worked without stopping to catch a breath. On the fourth day, the farm-owner took pity on the old man and gave him a nice, easy job sitting down sorting potatoes. That night the old fellow staggered in to announce, "I quit. I'm plum tuckered out." "But sorting potatoes is easy work," his employer observed. "It's not the work. It's making them durned decisions," the old man replied.

To add to your confusion, there are also new ways to use new products, new flavor twists, new combinations, variations and inspirations. But take heart. I've been there before you and have tried and tossed out many a mediocre mix and more-trouble-than-it's-worth "instant," and herewith present a lot of the best and the best of the lot, starting with "A" for appetizers, "B" for breakfasts, and, well, you'll see.

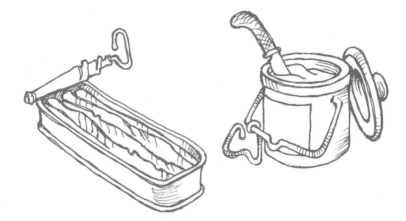

38

APPETIZERS OUGHT TO

Sooner or sooner, you're going to invite a few friends in for a drink. If newness is ever in order, it's now. Because the whole point and purpose of an appetizer is to appetize, pique, intrigue, titilate and tempt. You can't exactly expect a bowl of pretzels to do that.

It's hard to get ahead in the appetizer department, however, because whenever a clever hostess invents a new dip, an enter-prising manufacturer packages and purveys it. Which is fine with me. We can now have bacon dip without frying, onion dip with-out crying and clam dip without prying. So can our friends and neighbors. Considering the multiplicity of choice, however, it's unlikely we'll serve the same dip, dunk, goop or gunk on the same day of the week. Besides, we're going to provide something new to dip and dunk with. Instead of potato chips or crackers, serve raw cauliflower buds broken and sliced into flowerets, turnips or kohlrabi sliced paper thin and chilled in icewater, zucchini, aspar-agus tips, French endive.

Or you can buy a square of *cream cheese*. Plain. Unadorned. Pristine white. Plunk it on a pretty plate. Pour a jar of *red caviar* over the top. Serve with toasted white bread or party rye.

If you've never acquired a taste for caviar, your pocketbook will benefit. Unless you have other expensive tastes which most caviar-haters do. In fact, you won't even save money if you make this alternate cream cheese appetizer because it really isn't very good unless you make it with very good chutney. It's easy and delicious though. Just strew two or three tablespoons of very-good-*chutney* over a square of *cream cheese*. Serve with Melba toast.

Stuffed Gouda

Appetizers ought to appeal to the eye, too. A definite dazzler is stuffed Gouda. Buy a big, round, bright red Gouda cheese. Leave it out of the refrigerator overnight so that it is completely softened. Cut a caplike section off the top and scoop all the cheese out of the red covering. Leave a thin shell of cheese, so the whole keeps it shape. Mash the cheese you've removed with *2 tablespoons Worcestershire sauce, ½ teaspoon dry mustard, 2 tablespoons chopped onion* and *2 tablespoons mayonnaise.* Return the mixture to the red Gouda shell. Serve with whole wheat crackers.

You'll notice I haven't said anything about canapes. And I'm not going to. Canapes are for caterers. Because caterers have flocks of helpers to slather and spread. You have better things to do. And your guests will welcome having something to do with their hands. Besides, canapes, even the prettiest, tend to be disappointing. Because the minute they're made they start to wilt, and a wilted canape is worse than no canape at all.

Infinitely better is a bowl of spread and something to spread it on. Rules out limpness and solves the left-over problem. As anyone knows, there is practically nothing you can do with a left-over deviled ham canape. On the other hand, there are quite a lot of things you can do with a cup of left-over deviled ham. You can freeze it, make a sandwich of it, stuff a tomato with it, fill an omelet with it, pile it on an English muffin and pour cheese sauce over it. Well, you get the idea.

The most elegant spread you can serve also happens to be the best left-over. I'm talking about Steak Tartare and I keep hoping to have some left over. I never do. Somehow the most delicate, lavender-and-old-lace ladies turn into ravenous beasts when I serve my Steak Tartare. If I had some left over, I'd spread it on bread, slip it under the broiler, and enjoy.

Steak Tartare

This is fairly expensive, special-occasion stuff. But we were talking about parties, weren't we? And one beautiful appetizer is worth a dozen droopy, uneaten offerings. So. Supply yourself with ½ *pound round steak ground without fat*. It is absolutely necessary that absolutely all the fat be removed before the meat is ground. The only way to be absolutely sure that it is is to buy your round steak in one piece and have the butcher grind it, preferably before your eyes. Tell him what you're planning to make. He'll probably invite himself to dinner. What you do about that is your affair. What you do to the ground round is this. Add 2 *egg yolks, salt, pepper,* and 1 *teaspoon olive oil* and mix lightly with a fork. Mound the mixture on a plate and cover the top with a mixture of *minced parsley* and *chopped chives.* Garnish with *lemon wedges* and *capers.* About those capers, if there's a sophisticated man among your guests, don't skip them. To him, capers are essential to the Steak Tartare caper. Provide thin slices of rye and white bread or toast.

HEAT TREATMENTS

Nothing revs up the cocktail hour like arriving on the scene with a tray of piping hot hors d'oeuvres. Suddenly you're the center of attention. Adjured to get-'em-while-they're-hot, the most lethargic guest is galvanized into action. Oohs follow ahs. It's a party. Happily, hot appetizers are easy to do. Here are the newsiest of the new.

Peanutchuts

Spread squares of *white bread* with *peanut butter* (yes) top with *chutney* and a square of *bacon.* Broil till bacon crisps.

Hip Crab Dip

Mix a 12-ounce package cream cheese with 1 can drained crab meat. Mix in a few onion flakes and 1 teaspoon horseradish. Bake in a small casserole at 350° degrees for 20 minutes. Serve hot with crackers or triscuits.

Hot Cheese Puffs

Beat the white of 1 *egg* until stiff. Fold in ½ *cup grated cheese, salt, paprika* and 1 *teaspoon Worcestershire sauce.* Spread on *rounds of toast* (buy these in a box) and toast under the broiler 5 to 8 minutes, until puffed up and lightly brown.

FAST BREAK BREAKFASTS

The ultimate instant has to be instant breakfast. A meal in a glass. Stir, gulp, go. This may have been your modus operandi when you were single. Mornings with a man call for something more. Don't despair. Even if you're barely there before eleven, there are ways of creating bountiful, old-fashioned breakfasts.

Fruit First

Time was when you had to soak prunes for hours then simmer them lengthily. Now, just open a jar, spoon into your prettiest dish, add a squeeze of fresh lemon and serve. Ring in a variation now and then. Serve prunes hot. Combine them with whole canned apricots. Place a blanched almond or walnut in each prune cavity, wrap the prune with a thin slice of bacon, secure with a toothpick, broil till crisp.

42

There's nothing new about broiling half a grapefruit. There is when you top it with a spoonful of frozen orange concentrate first. Or pour on a splash of sherry. Or spoon on an adventurous dab of apple butter. Or raid the gourmet department for preserved lingonberries to spoon on cold after the broiling.

Bride's Breakfast Peaches

This is for your anniversary. Or for Valentine's Day. Or New Year's Day. Or your own special holiday. Half thaw *1 box quick-frozen peaches,* enough to make them eatable but still half-crystalized. Serve in sherbet glasses covered with pink champagne.

BLENDER SPLENDOR

Aren't you glad you're a bride in this day and age. When there are blenders extant. If you haven't one, start hinting. If you have one, make any and all of these morning marvels.

Pink Splendor

Whir in your blender: *½ package frozen strawberries, 1 cup crushed ice, ½ cup cream.* Pour in goblets and eat with a spoon.

Orange Splendor

Whir in your blender: *4 tablespoons frozen orange juice concentrate, ½ cup evaporated milk, 1 cup crushed ice.*

BREAD NEWS

Bread, rolls, muffins, biscuits, coffee cakes, popovers and more can be made from a mix. So find the baking-mix aisle and run amok. Your man will love you for it. Serve everything hot and if you feel super-luxurious, with unsalted butter spooned into an earthenware crock.

Sea Biscits au Gratin

If that's not enough variety for you, branch out with Sea Biscuits au Gratin. Brush large *sea biscuits* with *melted butter* and sprinkle with *grated cheese*. Set in the oven just long enough for the cheese to melt. Serve hot, of course.

Swiss Cheese Bread

Or begin with a loaf of unsliced *white bread*. Cut thick slices almost but not quite through to the bottom. Slip slices of *Swiss cheese* in each slot. Wrap in foil and heat in the oven.

Pop-up Breakfasts

Cinnamon toast happens in a hurry now that the sugar and cinnamon comes ready-mixed in a shaker-jar. Sprinkle on hot buttered toast or before the toasting. Slightly different effect. Get your man's vote as to which he likes best.

French toast, waffles and pancakes all come frozen. Pop them in the toaster and top with something interesting. Apple butter. Apricot jam. Sour cream and brown sugar. Sweet butter creamed with sugar and an ounce of Cointreau.

EASY EGGS

While there are mixes for making omelets and scrambled eggs, nothing beats Mother Nature's original product. The egg, itself. Perfectly packaged, the egg cooks in a matter of minutes. Unless you've a mind to, you need add nothing to it. And more often than not, the price is right.

So my advice would be to eschew mixes containing powdered eggs and go for the real thing prepared his way. Since the second most important thing for a bride to know might well be how-does-he-like-his-eggs, the thing to do is to find that out. It may be very easy. Which is to say he may refuse to eat even a forkful of an egg he deems grossly overdone and you would swear barely touched the pan. On the other hand, you may be blessed with the carefree kind of guy who says "any way" and means it. If your lad's the latter sort, you're home free. Otherwise you have a couple of choices. Learn to boil, scramble or fry his way, which may involve a good deal of trauma. Let him do it himself, which won't make you feel very important — a point women's lib tends to forget. Or you can convert those breakfast eggs into something exotic which he discovers he loves, doesn't know how to make and proves how clever he was to marry you.

Swiss Eggs

For each of you, put *1 slice Swiss cheese* in a custard cup. Set cups in the oven (350°) until the cheese begins to melt. Gently break *eggs* into custard cups. Try to keep the yolks whole. Sprinkle with *salt* and *pepper* and a fleck of *nutmeg*. Pour *2 tablespoons cream* into each cup, over the egg. Dot with *butter*. Bake until eggs are just set — 12 to 15 minutes.

Green-and-White Eggs

Hardboil *four eggs,* run them very briefly under cold water — just so you can handle them. You don't want the insides cool. Peel. Chop up with lots of *sweet butter,* a little *salt* and *pepper* and a couple of tablespoons of *fresh chopped parsley*. If you have *fresh chives,* snip a few in, too. Don't attempt to make this dish with dried herbs. The goodness depends on the freshness — of the eggs, butter and delicate greenery.

Eggs Benedict

Everybody knows that Eggs Benedict are the epitome of elegance. What you can hope to keep everybody from knowing is that you forehandedly supplied yourself with a package of *hollandaise sauce mix*. When the time comes to impress, which in my opinion is any and every time, toast an *English muffin,* lay a thin

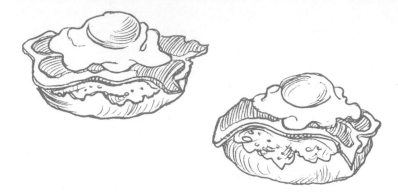

slice of *cooked ham* on top, put a *poached egg* on top of that and blanket with hollandaise sauce from a mix with a squeeze of *fresh lemon juice added*. Don't omit the lemon. It's what makes the whole thing plausible.

CAKES THAT TAKE THE

I continue to be grateful to Betty Crocker and her ilk for making it possible to ready a cake for the oven in 5 minutes and have only one bowl to wash. Admittedly carrot semolina soy cake is healthier than chocolate fudge cake. If anyone eats it. In my experience, hardly anyone does. In fact, I have a friend who serves such healthy food no one accepts her dinner invitations.

The point and purpose of having a husband, however, is to have him come home, and a fresh-baked, melt-in-the-mouth, honest-to-goodness gooey-icinged cake is hard to beat as an inducement. Whatever your man's favorite, it's likely to come in a package: Angel Food Cake, White Cake, Yellow Cake, Gingerbread, Orange Chiffon, Chocolate Cake, Lemon Pudding Cake, Coffee Cake, Pound Cake. It's quicker to make any of them than to list them. Withal, there remain interesting innovative things you can do with a package of cake mix.

46

Upside-down Cake

With almost any kind of *cake mix,* you can make almost any kind of upside-down cake. Melt *brown sugar* and *butter* in a cake

tin. Arrange slices of *canned pineapple, peaches, pears* or *apricots* in a pretty design, with or without a few cherries and nuts. Pour on cake batter and bake as directed. When you take the cake from the oven, invert the tin onto a cake plate, loose sides and turn out.

Coffee Cake

For an extra festive coffee cake, again begin with any *cake mix* you happen to have on hand. Pour half the batter into the pan. Sprinkle on half of the following mixture: *¾ cup light brown sugar, 2 teaspoons cinnamon, 1 cup chopped pecans.* Add the remaining batter. Sprinkle with the rest of the topping. Bake as directed. Serve warm.

Apricot Rum Cake

Cake mixes are not only short cuts, they're also regal routes to something spectacular like this. You'll need *1 package (1 lb. 8 oz.) orange-chiffon cake mix, 1 tablespoon grated orange peel, 1 table- spoon grated lemon peel.* (Try to grate fresh peel; it takes time, but look at all the time you're saving by using cake mix.)

Prepare cake mix as package label directs, adding orange and lemon peel with the *eggs* and *water*. Turn into ungreased 10-inch tube pan. Bake 45 to 55 minutes, or until surface springs back when gently pressed with fingertip. Invert pan immediately, hanging the tube over the neck of a bottle, if you haven't recycled all of yours already. Let the cake cool completely — about 1½ hours.

Meanwhile, make *Apricot Rum Syrup* this way: In a saucepan, combine *1 can* (12-ounce) *Apricot Nectar, ¾ cup sugar* and *1 cup water*. Bring to boiling, stirring until sugar is dissolved. Boil gently uncovered, 10 minutes, or until syrup measures about 2 cups. Remove from heat. Add *1 cup rum* and *¼ cup lemon juice*.

With a cake tester or a shish-kebab skewer or a Philips screwdriver borrowed from your husband's tool-box (put it back) make holes, 1 inch apart, in top of cake in pan. Pour warm syrup over cake, ¼ cup at a time, until all is used. Let stand at room temperature 2 hours or until all syrup is absorbed.

OTHER HINTS

If you've had a hard day at the office, missed a train, lost a glove, and found a parking ticket on your car and even a mix seems too much, you can still let him eat cake. Buy a *pound cake,* slice it lengthwise into lots of thin layers. Spread this filling between: *commercial sour cream* combined with *canned chocolate syrup.* A teaspoon of *rum* added is not amiss. Or buy a packaged supermarket *angel food cake.* Poke holes in it with a skewer and pour in a mixture of *Crème de Cacao* and *heavy cream.* Both these creations will taste even better the second day. And did you know, there are canned cakes? Eggnog. Chocolate. Lemon.

To say nothing of fruit cake, which seems uninspired around Christmas and dashingly different around the fourth of July.

HIS JUST DESSERTS

Single girls rarely serve desserts. That may be why they're single. Take heed. End your meals on the upbeat. Desserts may be kid stuff but there's a lot of small boy in most men.

As with most man-pleasing stratagems, it's best to keep your touch light. No slaving over a hot stove to come up with something heavy he feels he has to eat or he'll hurt your feelings. Just

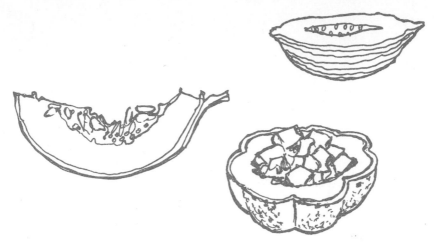

a taste of something wonderful, conjured up like magic, and enjoyed together with coffee and candlelight. Here's a whole month's worth of ideas.

1. Pear Helene. Add *½ teaspoon orange extract or Cointreau liqueur to chocolate sauce*. Pour over *canned pear halves*.

2. Rum Pumpkin Pie. Buy the pie. Heat in the oven. Pour on *4 tablespoons warmed rum*. Sprinkle with *nutmeg*.

3. Maple Sundae. Heat *maple syrup*. Pour on *butter pecan ice cream*.

6. Sour Grapes. Add *brown sugar* to *sour cream*. Mix with *seedless green grapes*.

7. Glazed Strawberry Tarts. Buy *tart shells*. Fill with *instant vanilla pudding*. Cover with *strawberries*. Melt *½ cup currant jelly* and pour over the berries. Chill.

8. Apple Whip. Into *2 stiffly beaten egg whites* beat *4 tablespoons confectioners' sugar*. Fold in *1 cup applesauce* and *¼ teaspoon nutmeg*.

9. Sunshine Parfait. Layer *orange sherbet, crushed pineapple* and *vanilla ice cream*.

10. Cheesecake. Buy a *graham cracker crumb crust*. Beat *one 8-ounce package cream cheese*, softened, with *½ cup sugar* until creamy. Blend in *one 4½-ounce container non-dairy whipped topping* thawed. Pour in crust. Chill at least 3 hours.

11. Pear Pair. Serve *pear-flavored yogurt* over *sliced pears*.

12. Cream Whip Amandine. Whip *½ cup cream*. Fold in *¼ cup sugar*, *1 tablespoon Grand Marnier liqueur* and *¼ cup toasted slivered almonds*. Let stand twenty minutes before chilling.

13. Banana saute. Fry peeled *bananas*, sliced in half, lengthwise, in *butter*. Sprinkle with *brown sugar*. Serve warm.

14. Mincemeat Ice Cream. Stir *1 tablespoon canned mincemeat* into *1 pint vanilla ice cream*.

15. Quick Baked Apples. Fill *canned baked apples* with *orange marmalade and chopped nuts*. Heat in 350° oven.

16. Toasted Chocolate Marshmallows. Top *marshmallows* with *chocolate bits*. Broil at least 4 inches from heat.

17. Rum Ricotta. To a cup of *Italian ricotta or creamed cottage cheese*, add *1 tablespoon cream*, *1 tablespoon sugar* and *1 tablespoon rum*. Blend smooth. Serve chilled, sprinkled with *cinnamon*.

18. Ambrosia. Cover *canned mandarin orange sections* with *Southern-style, moist pack coconut*.

19. Apricot Angel. Melt *1 cup apricot jam*. Pour over *angel food cake* slices toasted under the broiler.

20. Peachy Peaches. Thaw *a package of frozen peaches*. Pour into a baking dish. Cover with *sour cream*. Sprinkle with *brown sugar*. Place under broiler until sugar caramelizes.

21. South-of-the-border. Serve *cream cheese* with *guava jelly* and *crisp crackers*.

22. Vermont Cakes. Using a *pancake mix*, cook large, very thin pancakes. As they come from the griddle, cover each with *sweet butter* and *shaved maple sugar*.

23. Baked Banana Pudding. Fold *sliced bananas* into *vanilla pudding* made from a mix or canned. Bake in a slow oven (325°) 15 to 20 minutes.

50

24. Strawberries in Season. Serve *fresh berries* with their stems on, arranged in a circle around a little mound of *confectioners'* sugar. Dip and eat.

25. Caramelized Pineapple. Melt *butter* in a skillet. Add *canned pineapple chunks*, drained. Stir until lightly browned. Add *brown sugar* and continue heating and stirring until pineapple is caramel-

ized. Keep the heat low, and keep stirring. If you want to gild the lily you can serve this on vanilla ice cream.

26. Pink Devil. Serve bought *devil's food cake* with *strawberry ice cream* and *thawed frozen berries.*

27. Blue Melon. Serve *blueberries* in *honeydew melon* halves.

28. Apple Strudel. Buy *strudel* from the bake shop. Heat it in the oven, and just before serving, pour on *melted butter* and sprinkle with *sugar* and *cinnamon.* Tastes almost fresh-made.

29. Rum Fruit Cake. Thaw and drain a package of *frozen mixed fruit.* Sandwich it between slices of *sponge cake.* Sprinkle with *rum.* Let it mellow in the refrigerator at least an hour or two.

30. Chocolate Mint Brownies. Put *chocolate-covered peppermint patties* on top of bought *brownies.* Put them in a slow oven until the patties melt. Spread the resultant chocolate mint frosting around with a spatula. Serve warm.

51

MAIN CHANCES

With all this waxing enthusiastic about appetizers, breakfasts, and desserts, you may get the idea that I don't think much of ready-to-heat-and-eat main dishes. I don't. Elegant entrees purveyed by a restaurant or caterer are an exception. And exceptionally expensive. The main dish you pluck from your supermarket deep freeze is a horse of a different color and sometimes tastes like it. At best these entrees are disappointing. They don't look like the glorious colored pictures on the package. They say they serve two but if one of the two is a man, they don't. Which makes them twice as expensive as they appear to be. Sauces tend to be gluey, meat tends to be chewy and things like mushrooms turn out to be few and far between.

Besides, if your man has been a bachelor for any length of time, he's probably gone that gamut, from soupy stew to uninspired stroganoff. He married you hoping for something better. Give it to him.

You can without going back to the beginning. Take stew. As we were saying, there's not much to be said for most of the ready-mades, canned or frozen. There are short cuts. Here's one.

Short Cut Stew

Brown 2 *pounds* of respectable *beef* cut in decent-size chunks. This will make a lot of stew, which you should always make. To eat tomorrow and tomorrow, to freeze, or have a party with. Add

1 *can Golden Mushroom Soup,* undiluted and 1 *can dry red wine.* Now add 1 *package frozen vegetables* for stew — a colorful collection of whole onions, potatoes, leek, carrots and the like completely ready to pop in the pot with nary a peel left behind. Simmer for a couple of hours, adding water or wine but not too much, if it starts getting dry. Serve strewn with chopped fresh parsley.

Quick Chicken Blanquette

Most frozen or canned creamed chicken dishes tend to be unluxurious because they proffer more sauce than chicken. To reverse this situation, pour *two cans chicken gravy,* or *two cups sauce* made from a mix, into a casserole with a tight cover. Put in two *chicken legs or breasts* or one of each. No, you don't have to brown the chicken first. In fact, not-browning is what makes it Blanquette — a lovely white-white entree. It also saves time and absolves you from having to scrub a skillet. Bake, covered, in 350° oven for 50 minutes. Again a ready-made — sauce — has saved the day with no one the wiser, especially if you add a smidgeon of *sherry* before serving or stir in a spoonful of *sour cream* after the Blanquette's out of the oven.

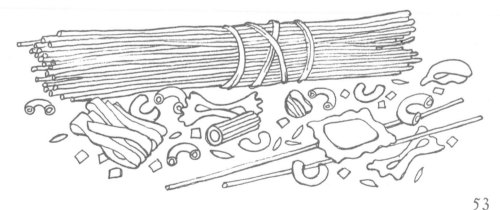

Potatoes, Pasta, Noodles and Rice

Eat 'em while you're young. Some day they'll be off-limits. In the interim, the good news is that the pre-seasoned, quick-cooking versions of these old favorites are almost all good. The mashed potatoes leave something to be desired, but you were making them to pour gravy over anyway, weren't you? Just be sure to have good gravy. Macaroni and rice mixes, on the other hand, tend to be terrific. Make according to directions and lily-gild at will. With more cheese, fresh-grated, slivered almonds, pine nuts, or good old fresh chopped parsley. When I say chopped, I really mean snipped. Those scissors I was campaigning for early on are a bride's best friend when it comes to parsley. Chopping parsley calls for a board which you have to wash off, and a sharp knife with which you could cut yourself. And somehow, it all seems too much trouble. With scissors, you just hold a sprig of parsley over the dish and snip away until you have a pretty dusting of garden greenery.

UNSTUFFY STUFFING

Stuffing is something I don't make from scratch anymore. True, it's a way to use up stale bread, but it's easier not to let the bread get stale in the first place. And while some stuffing is crumby and some comes in cubes, it's all pretty good. Flavorings vary so you may have to cast about a bit to find your own special favorite. When you do, there are a number of interesting main-dish things you can do with it. You can, for example, make up a batch of stuffing according to package directions and press it against the sides of a pie tin, forming a shell, into which you then pour frozen creamed vegetables, cooked according to the directions on their package.

You can cook any meat, fish or fowl on a bed of stuffing. You can sandwich stuffing between ham slices, and bake. You can sprinkle the crumbly kind on casseroles and toss the cube kind, dry, into salads. You can mix it with chopped beef to make meatballs. You can use it to bread fish or veal. Use the crumb type. Dip fish or veal in beaten egg, then in stuffing mix. Saute and serve. No seasoning needed.

NOT BY BREAD ALONE

Refrigerated biscuits and rolls can turn into main events when they join up with meat. For lunch, brunch or midnight supper, serve *Pigs In Blankets*. Wrap refrigerated biscuit dough around frankfurters or sausages and bake. For the ultimate in elegance, make *Beef Wellington* this easy way. Partially roast a filet of beef, spread top and sides with pate. Open a can of refrigerated crescent dinner rolls. Separate rolls, place crosswise over top and down sides, overlapping slightly. Bake 15 minutes more. Serve with marchand de vin sauce — page 16.

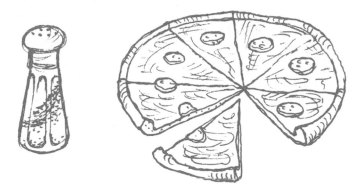

Pizza

You can also use refrigerated crescent dinner rolls to make an almost-home-made *Pizza*. Oil a pizza pan. Open two packages *crescent rolls*. Fit triangles of dough into pizza pan. Spread *1 can spaghetti sauce* on top. Sprinkle *1 can sliced mushrooms* on top of that, and a pinch of *oregano* on top of them. Sprinkle *½ package shredded mozzarella cheese* over all. Bake in a hot oven (400°) for 20 minutes until crusts are brown.

OTHER CONTENDERS

For quick reference, here are a few more handy-to-have-on-hand convenience foods.

Frozen chopped onions. Why cry when you don't have to?

Dry onion soup mix. Count on it. Tomorrow someone will tell you still another thing you can do with dry onion soup mix. That's why I'm not going to.

Dried mushrooms. Expensive but they keep forever and taste much better than frozen or canned. Of course, they look like something to conjure black magic with so hide them unless you think a little mystery will add to your allure.

Chopped frozen spinach. Does anybody chop spinach anymore? I don't know. I do know, and you may want to, that anything "Florentine" means with spinach. I also know and commend to you the truth that chopped spinach makes a sophisticated stuffing for fish, chicken, tomatoes and ham.

Dry mixes for gravy and sauce. Gussy them up with mushrooms, chopped parsley and wine.

Canned gravy and sauce. Ditto.

Canned French fried onion rings. Good for garnish any old time.

Canned or packaged moist-pack shredded coconut. For unsweet things, buy unsweetened coconut in a health store. Pour hot milk over it, let stand 30 minutes and strain through a sieve. Use when your recipe calls for coconut milk. Or put a chicken in a covered casserole and bake an hour, basting with the coconut milk you've made. That'll make 'em sit up and take notice. Old Portuguese recipe. They use garlic and lemon juice to marinate the chicken first. You can but you don't have to.

Something Borrowed

Here we go. Around the world with knife, fork and spoon, and chopsticks. Let's begin close to home. With specialties from Nassau in the Bahamas.

NICE THINGS FROM NASSAU

Peas 'n Rice

You've heard the song. "Mama don' want no peas 'n rice, no coconut oil." Here's what it's all about. To serve 8, you'll need to brown a *chopped onion* in *2 tablespoons shortening.* Add *2½ cups canned tomatoes,* and "fry down" as the natives say, till thick. Add *1 teaspoon thyme* and place in a deep pot. Add *1 cup canned pigeon peas, 1 cup water* and pinch of *salt.* Bring mixture to a boil and then add *2 cups rice.* Stir with a fork, cooking slowly until dry.

Tropic Salad

Peel and dice a *cantaloupe* and mix it with *1 cup miniature marshmallows, 2 large bananas,* sliced, and *½ cup pecans,* shelled, natch. Now mix *½ cup strawberry ice cream* with *½ cup mayonnaise* and mix this in with the fruit. Serve on *greens* to six people.

Grapefruit Surprise

Make *pie crust* from a mix. Roll it to fit your pie pan, but don't put it in the pan. Instead, butter the pie pan and fill it with *grapefruit sections* — about *2½ cups.* Now mix *¾ cup light brown sugar, 1 tablespoon flour* and *1 tablespoon melted butter.* Sprinkle this over the grapefruit. Top with pie pastry and bake in 325° oven for 25 minutes. Surprise 8.

FROM ITALY WITH LOVE

Veal and Anchovies

Buy *veal cutlets* for two or if you're feeling hospitable, for four. Have your butcher pound it thin. If he won't, use the edge of a saucer. Butter a casserole. Line the bottom with the veal. Cut up a few *anchovies* and sprinkle them on top. Add a clove of *garlic,* cut fine, if you're a garlic-lover. The dish will survive but it won't be authentic without. Add *1 can tomato sauce.* Sprinkle a lot of *Parmesan cheese* over that. Cover and bake at 350° for ¾ hour. Take out and cover with slices of *mozzarella cheese.* Put it back in the oven uncovered until the mozzarella melts, bubbles and maybe gets a little brown. Serve with plain spaghetti and a green salad and wine.

A word of warning. Don't tell your restauranteur that you make Veal and Anchovies. He'll start coming to your place.

Fettucini

Cook *fettucini* according to package directions — al dente — or just barely tender. Drain. At the table in a chafing dish or electric skillet, melt ½ pound butter. Stir in 2 *tablespoons heavy cream*. Add the drained fettucini. Pour freshly grated *Parmesan cheese* over all — a cup should do it, but it must be freshly grated. Toss as if you were tossing a salad until every strand is coated. A twist of *fresh pepper* would not be amiss. Serve with a big green salad and fruit and wine.

Francesca's Special Sicilian Cheesecake

To make this, you'll need a spring-form cake tin. Beg, borrow, or buy, but don't try to do without. What's a spring form cake tin? Essentially, it's expandable — so you can get the cake out, whole and handsome. In addition, you'll need: one 3-pound can ricotta cheese, 8 egg yolks, 2 cups sugar, ½ cup flour, the grated rind of *one lemon, 1 teaspoon vanilla, 8 egg whites,* and some *graham cracker crumbs.*

Begin by separating the eggs. You know, don't you, that if you get the tiniest speck of yolk in with the whites, they won't beat up stiff? O.K. take care. There's a fair amount of beating involved here, so you'll be happier with an electric mixer of some sort. The small hand-type is fine. So: Beat the ricotta until it's smooth. Gradually add 1½ cups sugar and the egg yolks, beating after each addition. Beat in the flour, lemon rind and vanilla. With *clean* beaters, whip the egg whites with ½ cup sugar. Fold the egg white mixture into the ricotta mixture and pour into a 12″ spring form pan which has been well-buttered and sprinkled with graham cracker crumbs. Bake in preheated 425° oven for 10 minutes; lower temperature to 350° and bake for one hour. Turn off heat and allow to cool in oven.

CHINESE SPECIALTIES

Sooner or later, if you like Chinese food and love to cook, you're going to want a wok. Don't ask questions now. When you've reached that point in your culinary evolution, you'll know exactly what a wok is and why you want one. In the interim, it's quite possible to get a taste of Chinese cooking at home, using whatever pots and pans you happen to have at hand. In fact, you can even prepare a dish which the Chinese serve as the star of a banquet.

Orange Leek Duck

The first time I saw a Chinese cook prepare this dish, I almost gave up the idea of ever emulating him. He began by removing the peel of an orange with a wrist-snap and a sharp knife, in one continuous spiral. I was quite sure I could never do that. I was quite right. I can't. But I have discovered it is not necessary. What is necessary is to peel *2 oranges* and save the peel. Cut through and remove the white part and membrane around the orange. Then slice the orange into thin slices. Now place a *Long Island duckling* — about 4 pounds — on a rack in a roasting pan. Add *2 cups*

water to the pan. Roast in 350° oven for an hour. Now and again, toward the end of the roasting time, prick the skin of the duck to let the fat run out. Now mix together *¼ cup soy sauce, ½ cup dry sherry* and *2 cups leek* cut in 2 inch pieces. Do this in a Dutch oven or large covered kettle. Place the duck on top, breast side up. Bring to boil. Add *2½ cups water,* bring to boil again, and lower heat to simmer, covered, 30 minutes. Spoon the juices up over the duck and simmer 30 minutes more. Now for the orange peel — spirals or whatever shape you've managed to carve. Stuff it into the cavity of the duck. Pour *2 tablespoons dark corn syrup* over the duck, and cook 1 hour more, basting at least once. Remove cover and cook ten minutes more. Serve on platter surrounded by orange slices. Simmer the juices a few minutes more and pour them over the duck.

Chinese Roast Pork

Serve hot or cold, as a main course or as hors d'oeuvres.

Begin by making a marinating sauce. Combine these things in a large flat pan: *6 slices fresh ginger root* if you can obtain them; *2 stalks green onions* cut in pieces; *2 cloves garlic* crushed; *6 table-spoons sherry; 3 tablespoons catsup; 3 tablespoons chili sauce; 3 tablespoons corn syrup* and *1 teaspoon salt.* Cut *3 pounds lean pork tenderloin* or pork butt into strips. Put in the sauce to mari-nate overnight. Brush with *honey* and arrange on a rack. Bake in 350° oven for 35 minutes. Turn heat to 450° and bake 15 minutes longer. Remove from oven, cool slightly or completely and dice.

SCANDINAVIAN DELIGHTS

Kale Soup

If you're Danish you'll call it Gronnkalsuppe. If you're Finnish, you'll call it Lehtikaalisosekeitto. If you're Norwegian, you'll call it Gronnkalsuppe. If you're Swedish, you'll call it Gronkalsoppa. And if you're a soup fan, you'll call for it often.

Wash some *kale* — about half a big plant — and drain the water off. Cook in *salted* water for ten minutes. Strain. Save the liquid. Chop the kale with *¼ cup chives.* Melt *1 tablespoon but-ter,* stir in *1½ tablespoons flour.* When it's smooth, add the liquid

you've saved. Stir. Simmer. Add kale and chives and reheat. Serve with *hard boiled eggs* cut in sections. 4 servings.

Sailor's Stew

Cut *1½ pounds beef chuck* into ¼″ thick slices and pound them slightly. Peel *6 medium potatoes* and cut them in thick slices. Heat *2 tablespoons butter* in a skillet, saute *3 medium onions* sliced and brown the meat on both sides. In a casserole, layer potatoes, meat, and onions, sprinkling with salt and pepper. Pour *1½ cups boiling water* into the skillet, stir and add liquid to casserole. Add *½ cup beer.* Cover and cook in moderate oven, 375°, 1 hour or until meat is tender. Sprinkle with *chopped parsley* just before serving. Serves 4.

Troll Pudding

Beat *3 egg whites* until stiff. Add *1 cup lingonberry preserves* — or if you have to, cranberry preserves — along with *1 teaspoon vanilla* and *2½ tablespoons sugar.* Beat until light and fluffy. Serves 6.

Fylte Stekte Epler
Norwegian Stuffed Baked Apples

Mix *½ cup blanched, ground almonds* with *¼ cup sugar* and *2 tablespoons water* to make a paste. Peel *8 big, tart apples,* and

core them. Fill centers with almond paste. Roll apples in melted *butter* and then in *unseasoned bread crumbs* mixed with *sugar*. Bake in buttered baking dish in 425° oven about 25 minutes. Serve with *whipped cream*. 8 servings.

FONDUE FROM SWITZERLAND
or what to do with a wedding present

Fondue pots are so pretty and gay people just can't resist giving them as wedding presents. So chances are you've received one. What to do with it? Use it for appetizers, main meals and desserts. But begin with the classic Swiss Fondue made this way. Rub the fondue pot with *garlic,* pour in 1½ *cups dry white wine* and warm over medium heat but do not boil. Add 2 *cups grated imported Swiss cheese* and 2 *cups grated imported Gruyere,* stirring constantly with a wooden spoon until cheese is completely melted and the mixture just starts to bubble. You know, don't you, that if you stir in a figure eight, you manage to cover the ground most effectively? Now combine 2 *tablespoons cornstarch* with ½ *cup kirsch* and *a dash of salt, pepper* and *nutmeg.* Gradually add this to the cheese mixture, still stirring constantly. Keep at low heat and serve with cubes of crusty *French bread.* Guests spear bread cubes, dip into the fondue, and enjoy. If a guest loses his bread cube, he or she pays with a kiss. Who says the Alps are cold?

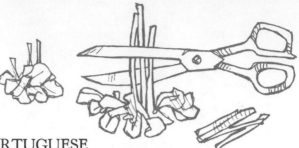

FROM THE PORTUGUESE

Green Soup

Cook *ten small, red-skinned potatoes,* peeled, in water and a pinch of *salt,* in a covered pot until very tender. Put the potatoes, water and all, through a food mill. Return to saucepan. Add 2 *tablespoons olive oil* and bring to a boil. Add 2 *cups* washed and trimmed watercress leaves (shake leaves to remove moisture). Cook two minutes. Serves six.

SCOTLAND HO

Shortbread

Make a mouth-watering Scottish Shortbread this way. Knead together 1 *cup flour, 1 cup very soft butter,* ½ *cup sugar,* ½ *cup ground almonds.* Roll it out into a circle, half an inch thick. Prick it with a fork. Mark it in pie-shaped wedges. Bake in 325° oven for 1½ hours.

SWISS ENCHILADAS FROM MEXICO

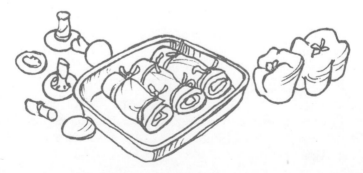

Anything with cream in it is called "Swiss" in Mexico. Anyone with gourmet tastes calls this dish delicious. If you use frozen or canned tortillas, it's quick to make. And authentic as it is, it won't burn your tongue off with hot spices.

Saute some *chopped onion* in *oil*. Add 1 *crushed garlic clove* and 2 *cups tomato puree*, 2 *chopped canned green chilies* and 2 *cups cooked, diced chicken*. Season with *salt* and *pepper* and simmer ten minutes. Fry a *dozen tortillas* in hot *oil*. Don't crisp them because you're going to roll them up in a minute or two. *Dissolve 6 bouillon cubes* in 3 *cups hot cream*. Dip each tortilla in this, cover generously with chicken filling and roll up. Arrange the rolls in a baking dish and pour the remaining cream mixture over them. Top with ½ *pound grated Swiss cheese*. Bake in 350° oven for 30 minutes.

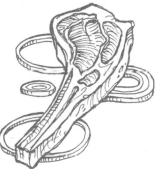

AUSTRALIAN CHOPS DOWN-UNDER

Put some nice plump *lamb chops* in a baking pan with a little fat. On each chop put *salt* and *pepper,* a thin *slice onion,* a slice of your favorite *cheese,* and 1 *tablespoon sour cream*. Bake in a moderate oven for half hour or so until golden brown. When cooked, strain off juice and add a little more cream to it and serve it separately in a gravy dish.

65

HUNGARIAN HOT POT

You'll need 1 ½ *pounds lean leg of pork* or *pork shoulder* and about 2 hours — cooking time, not preparation time. In a plastic bag, combine *flour, paprika* — a good two tablespoonsful — and *salt.* Shake meat in bag to coat evenly. In a large (4-quart) sauce pot or Dutch oven, with a tight-fitting cover, brown *2 tablespoons finely chopped onion* in *2 tablespoons fat.* Add contents of plastic bag. Brown meat on all sides. Add *2 tablespoons hot water.* Cover pot and simmer 1 hour, stirring occasionally. Add some water if it gets too dry. Add a *number 2½ can* (about 3½ cups) *sauerkraut,* along with *2 cups hot water.* Bring to a boil and simmer ½ hour longer. Remove from heat and blend in *1½ cups thick sour cream.* Do not boil. Serve in bowls.

FABULOUS FRENCH DISHES

Don't let French cooking inhibit you. There is a lot to French cooking. But you don't have to master the art. Dabbling will do very deliciously for a start. A few impressive culinary feats and the rumor will go round that you are a fabulous French cook. Whether or not you go on to become one is up to you. Here are the recipes you need to start.

Coquilles St. Jacques

Provide yourself with *four or five scallops per person.* Cut the scallops in two and chop *four or five shallots.* If you're serving six or so, put a third of a pound of *butter* into a frying pan and fry the scallop pieces for ten minutes. Add the shallots. Continue cooking five minutes more. Don't overcook. Remove the pan from the heat. Transfer scallops to warm plate. Add *4 tablespoons dry white wine* to pan. Return to heat and stir around to dissolve everything in the bottom of the pan. Add *1½ cups cream.* Continue cooking 5 minutes more at reduced heat. Add *salt* and *pepper.* Add *scallops.* Serve in scallop shells if you have them.

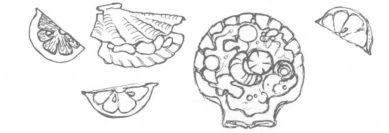

Blanquette de Veau

This takes time to tell, but it's actually easy to make. Put *2 pounds veal cubes* in a large pan and cover with cold water. Bring slowly to a boil and skim off what rises to the top. We're not going to call it scum, though that's what it's called. No matter, the end result is delectable. Add *salt, 1 onion,* a couple of sliced *carrots,* a *bay leaf* and a bit of *thyme,* a *clove* if you feel like it. Cover and cook slowly for 1½ hours. At the same time cook *12 fresh mushrooms* in *butter* and in another pan, *12 small onions in butter.* Now make a cream sauce by doing this: In a small pan, melt *⅓ cup butter,* stir in *3 tablespoons flour.* Add *1 cup cream,* stir until thickened and smooth. Add two tablespoons of this mixture to *2 beaten egg yolks,* then carefully stir this mixture back into the cream sauce. When well blended, add a bit of veal stock — liquid from the cooking pot — and stir over low heat until you have lots of creamy smooth sauce. Don't let it boil. Just before serving, add the *juice of 1 lemon* and some *chopped parsley.* Place the veal in a warm dish and pour the cream sauce over it.

Coq au Vin

To serve six, begin with *2 chickens,* cut up. Sprinkle the pieces with *salt, pepper* and *flour.* Now dice — that means cut up in tiny squares — *6 slices bacon.* Throw the bacon in a large heavy frying pan with about *20 tiny onions* and the chicken. Saute until golden brown. If you like *garlic,* put in a clove, chopped, at this point, with *½ cup brandy.* Cook about 1 minute. Now pour *1 bottle red wine* over all and cook over low heat, covered, about 30 minutes.

Add ½ *pound mushrooms* and continue cooking, covered, about 15 minutes longer. Remove chicken to platter. Mix a little *flour* with *cold water* and add to skillet, cook, stirring until thickened. Pour over the chicken. Sauteed bread triangles and parsley are traditional garnish.

Coeur à la Crème

What more bride-like dessert than a heart-shaped one? If you have the fantastic good fortune to own a heart-shaped wicker basket, use it to make Coeur à la Creme. If not, use a sieve or colander — and buy a heart-shaped wicker basket the first time you see one. Pretty wall decor and nice heaped with fruit or flowers as a centerpiece. Here's how to make this most traditional of French desserts — in strawberry season, because this is one time when frozen berries really won't do.

Beat together ½ *pound cream cheese* and ½ *pound cottage cheese,* drained. Gradually add *1 cup heavy cream*. Continue beating until smooth. Line your basket, sieve or colander with wet cheesecloth, place over a deep bowl and pour in the cheese mixture. Refrigerate overnight so it can drain. To serve, turn out onto a pretty dish, surround with *strawberries* and open some champagne.

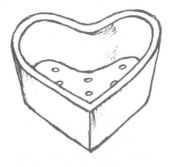

Bride's-Eye View

THE PENNYWISE BRIDE

By the time you get good at economizing on food, you probably won't need to. This little irony of life is reversible, however, because while experience is the best teacher, it doesn't have to be your own experience. Here are the facts and fantasies I've learned about cooking niftily and thriftily.

Begin at the beginning. In the market. Foodstores are full of non-food items. Buy as few of these as possible. I almost never buy wax paper or plastic freezer wrap, because so many things come in plastic bags. Our newspaper even comes plastic-bagged. I take the paper out, pop a few chops or muffins in, twist the top shut or tape it airtight. You can use the giant plastic bags your dry cleaner provides in much the same way, cutting it into handy squares which you store in a drawer. Bread wrappers, frozen vegetable bags, save and use them all.

Don't buy paper towels. It's better for the ecology to use cloth. Of course, you won't iron your dish towels, but you were going to the laundromat anyway, weren't you?

69

I don't buy paper napkins, either. Use colored ones of no-iron fabric — fingertip terry towels are especially nice. Buy two good-looking napkin rings. Your table will look prettier and your food money will go farther.

You can save money on sauces by avoiding sauce-mixes and making your own. If you need to save time as well as money, make a big batch of inexpensive white sauce mix, store it in the refrigerator and vary it all manner of ways. Here's how.

WHITE SAUCERY

Put *1 cup flour, 4 cups instant nonfat dry milk granules,* and *4 teaspoons salt* into a bowl. Add *1 cup butter* or margarine, cut up. Work the butter into the flour mixture with your fingers or a pastry blender. Put it in a glass jar with a tight cover and store it in the refrigerator.

For thin white sauce, use ⅓ cup mix and 1 cup milk; for medium sauce, use ½ cup mix and 1 cup milk; for thick sauce, use 1 cup of mix and 1 cup of milk.

Boil gently, stirring constantly, until thickened — about 2 minutes.

Variations:

Add 1 teaspoon dillweed or chopped dill. Good on fish.

Add 2 tablespoons prepared horseradish. Good on boiled beef.
Add 2 tablespoons dark prepared mustard. Good on smoked pork.
Add 1 teaspoon curry powder. Good with eggs, chicken or rice.
Add three tablespoons grated Parmesan and three tablespoons grated Gruyere cheese. Stir in ¼ cup light cream. Good for eggs or noodles.
Add 1 can sliced mushrooms and 2 diced pimentos. Good over diced poultry or hard-cooked eggs.

Soup from Sauce

Use this mix to make soup. Combine ⅓ cup mix with 1 cup milk. Add ½ cup cooked chopped spinach or broccoli, or tomato puree, or a can of cream-style corn, or a can of minced clams, undrained.

FRESH VEGETABLE SECRETS

Buy celery, cabbage and carrots fresh. Frozen carrots are costly, and canned carrots don't taste very good. Celery and cabbage are good or bad buys depending on the time of year. You can sometimes acquire a giant head of cabbage for 6¢. Other times it may cost 39¢. Cauliflower prices fluctuate even more wildly. Buy when it's low — less than 20¢ a head — and when it's high, pass it by. Frozen cauliflower's uneconomical, and rubbery to boot. Frozen peas, on the other hand, are usually a better buy than fresh ones. Unless you need the pods for your compost heap. Frozen chopped spinach also can be a very good buy if you buy it when it's on sale. The cheapest canned vegetables are beets and tomatoes. Buy other canned vegetables only when they're on sale and then stock up. Never buy fresh asparagus except at the height of the season. It's fairly expensive even then but it tastes so delicate and green and fresh, it's worth a once-a-year splurge.

Besides being economical if you buy in season, fresh vegetables pay a dividend in vitamins. So you may end up saving money on doctor bills, too. Raw green vegetables stay fresh in the refrigerator for at least a week. Potatoes, squash and onions generally last about two weeks without refrigeration.

If you think fresh vegetables are a lot of trouble to prepare, you're right. If you don't know a secret I'm about to impart.

71

It's a one-word secret, really. Oven. That's right. Cook fresh vegetables in the oven. It's easy. It seems to enhance the flavor so you needn't bother with sauces and such. And the vegetables come out looking downright beautiful.

Here's the whole how-to. Start with a casserole with a tight-fitting cover. Add a cup of liquid, no more. Usually half a cup is enough. Use water, juice or wine. Bake vegetables at 350° until tender. Potatoes, squash or carrots take longer than green vegetables. You can peel your vegetables if you wish, but you save vitamins and time if you don't. A thorough scrubbing will usually do. For variety, add herbs, cheese and other frivolities. Suggestions? Try these.

Creative Carrots

Use several large carrots, whole or cut in half lengthwise. Add *½ cup orange juice, ½ cup water, 1 teaspoon sugar.* Sprinkle with *ground cinnamon* and *allspice.* Cover. Bake.

Broccoli

Cut up a bunch of *broccoli,* wash it and put it in your casserole.

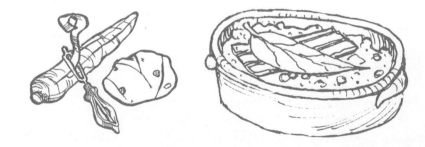

Add several small *onions,* two *new potatoes* in their skins, *1 cup beef* or *chicken broth.* Cover. Bake.

Mushroom Medley

Grease your casserole and make alternate layers of *fresh sliced mushrooms* dipped in *flour, potatoes,* sliced and dipped in flour, *onions* sliced and dipped in *flour.* Add *1 cup milk.* Sprinkle on *rosemary* and *thyme.* Cover. Bake.

Acorn Squash

Cut *squash* in half and scoop out seeds. Place in casserole with *½ cup water* and *½ cup maple syrup.* Cover. Bake.

CHICKEN COMES FIRST

Never mind which came first, the chicken or the egg, both tend to be good buys. Buy both often and collect interesting recipes to keep variety in your life. Here are a few good ones to start. We'll assume the chicken came first.

Definitely Different Chicken

Saute a couple of strips of *bacon.* Take them out of the skillet and save them. In the same fat, saute *½ cup chopped onion* with *1 teaspoon dried tarragon.* Sprinkle *salt* and *paprika* on *chicken pieces,* dip in *flour,* and saute in the same skillet. Remove to casserole. Pour fat in skillet over chicken in casserole. Add *1½ cups burgundy wine,* 8 *pitted prunes,* 4 *dates,* seeded and chopped, *½*

cup raisins or if they're in season, seedless white grapes. Cover. Bake in 350° oven for 45 minutes. Take the cover off and continue baking about ten minutes more.

Lemon Chicken

Flour, salt and *pepper* a cut-up frying *chicken*. Place it in a casserole with small lumps of *butter,* thin slices of *lemon* and *onion.* Another layer of chicken. Another of lemon and onion. No liquid. Bake in 350° oven 1 hour uncovered. Ten minutes before serving pour ½ *pint cream* over chicken. Cover. Cook ten minutes more.

Most Inexpensive Chicken Casserole

No cream. No wine. Yet it tastes delicious. Place cut-up *fryer* in casserole in layers, sprinkling each layer with *flour.* Put 4 *tablespoons flour* in a cup and fill the cup with water. Stir. Pour this over the chicken. Add *salt, paprika, 2 tablespoons Worcestershire sauce* and *2 bay leaves.* Cover. Bake one hour at 350°.

Charcoal-Broiled

Really do it on charcoal. In the fireplace, on the back porch, in the park. Dramatic, delicious, different. Just build your fire, let it

die down to embers. Grease the grill and broil the chicken slowly, basting from time to time with melted butter or margarine. Not necessary, but fun: throw a handful of rosemary or thyme on the coals.

Italian Chicken

Place a cut-up *fryer* in a casserole with a can of *spaghetti sauce*. Brown the chicken in a skillet, first, if you have time, but all will be well if you don't.

Hawaiian Chicken

Saute a cut-up *chicken* in a deep skillet. Add *1 can chicken gravy* and *½ cup drained frozen or canned pineapple chunks*. Cover and simmer forty minutes or until tender. A sprinkle of *cinnamon* would not be amiss at serving time.

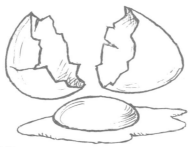

THEN THE EGG

I have been told that the most elegant meal in the world consists of a perfectly made omelet and a glass of champagne. Omit the champagne and you save a great deal of money.

The Perfect Omelet

As for making a perfect omelet, that's easy. And it takes about 3 minutes. Which dictates doing it when everything else is done. Mix *salt, pepper, 3 eggs* and *3 tablespoons cold water* together with a fork. You don't have to beat it forever, just till it's foamy and light. Heat a tablespoon of butter in a skillet, pour in egg mixture, reduce heat slightly, but cook eggs quickly. As the mixture begins to thicken, lift the edges with a spatula and let the

75

uncooked portions run underneath. Keep doing this, tilting the skillet to hasten the flow of uncooked egg. When eggs are set and the surface is still moist, fold in half. Slide onto a hot plate. Serve with something interesting in the way of breadstuffs.

Fill before Folding

You can fill an omelet with all manner of things. Left-over creamed chicken, flaked tuna, creamed chopped spinach, snippets of ham, cheese, or for dessert, apricot, plum or strawberry jam.

Creamed Eggs

Hard boil as many eggs as you're in the mood for. Pour hot *white sauce* made from your own mix (page 70) over all. Sprinkle with *Parmesan cheese*. Of course, you know how to hard-boil eggs. Well, a good way is to put the eggs in a pan, cover with cold water to at least 1 inch above the eggs. Bring water to boiling. Turn off heat and let stand 20 minutes. Cool promptly with cold water. This cooling is important. It makes the shells easier to re-move and prevents a darkness around the rims of the yolks which doesn't hurt but doesn't look very cheery. I have a cook book that tells you how to remove the shells of hard boiled eggs. With your fingers. I figure if you don't know how to get the shell off a hard-boiled egg, you're probably not a bride at all. Men like helpless girls but not that helpless.

French Toast

An elegant, inexpensive brunch dish or dessert is made by beat-ing 2 *eggs* with 1 *tablespoon water*. Melt some *butter* in a skillet. Dip slices of bread into the egg mixture, and then saute them slowly in the butter. Serve with *maple syrup* heated with *butter* and a hint of *nutmeg*.

Super Scramble

Serve this when you have unexpected company. Men like it, and it won't wreck the budget. For the mushrooms, choose cans labeled "stems and pieces" — less expensive than whole mushrooms and every bit as good for this recipe.

Saute some *chopped onion* in *butter*. Add *1 can tomato paste, 1 can pimentos*, cut up, *1 can mushrooms*, (drained) and *2 tablespoons olive oil*. Beat *6 eggs* with *1 cup milk*, some *salt* and *pepper*, and if you like it, some *garlic powder*. Pour it into the skillet with the tomato-mushroom mixture and cook it all together, scrambling it with a fork as much or as little as you've a mind to. Don't overcook. Serve on toasted English muffins or Holland rusks.

Candlelight Eggs

This is as elegant as filet mignon, half as expensive, and incredibly easy to make. It tastes as if a French chef had been slaving over the sauce all day. Do serve on your prettiest plates. At midnight by candlelight? I would.

Saute some *mushrooms* in *butter*. Spoon on a blanket of *sour cream*. Use the whole container. This whole meal will still cost not much more more than a dollar. Make indentations in the cream for however many *eggs* you're having. Break the eggs in. Sprinkle with *paprika*. Cover. Cook gently until eggs are set. Lay slices of *Swiss cheese* on top and slide under the broiler till the cheese melts.

77

FRUITFUL SAVINGS

The cheapest canned fruits are applesauce and peaches. Concentrate on these because they're very versatile and buy others only on sale. Then stock up. They last a long time. When you use a can of fruit, drain the syrup into a large jar and keep it in the refrigerator. Use this juice mixed with mayonnaise for fruit salad dressing. Thicken it with cornstarch and pour it over stale cake. Combine it with a bit of margarine and brown sugar as a glaze for ham or cooked carrots. Use it to baste chicken. Use it instead of water when you make gelatin dessert.

Oh, Applesauce

Serve chilled *applesauce* in a crystal bowl, topped with *whipped cream* and shavings of *bitter chocolate*.

Mix a few tablespoons of *maple syrup* into *applesauce* and serve warmed.

Serve chilled *applesauce* over *hot gingerbread*.

Cream *butter, flour, brown sugar* and *cinnamon* together. Put on top of *applesauce* and bake in 350° oven till topping is crisp.

Serve, sparked with *lemon juice,* as an accompaniment for pork.

Fill baked *tart shells* with *applesauce* and top with *meringue*.

Serve with *pancakes* instead of syrup.

Peach Possibilities

Place *peaches* in a shallow baking pan with ¼ *cup juice*. Spread them with ¼ *cup brown sugar, 1 tablespoon butter* and *1 tablespoon brandy*. Bake ten or fifteen minutes in 350° oven.

Drain *peach halves*. Fill the cavities with sherry. Chill. Serve with *whipped cream*.

Broil *peach halves* and serve with chicken or ham. Fill first with *cranberry sauce* or *marmalade,* if you're feeling extra festive.

THE NATURAL BRIDE

NATURAL FOOD ISN'T NEW

There's nothing new about natural food. Eve served it. But a lot has happened to the apple since then. Some good: pie. Some bad: chemical preservatives, artificial flavorings. If you're into natural food, you're up on your soapbox shouting. If you're not, and a friend has slipped you a dry, dog-biscuit-of-a-health food, you're running as fast as you can the other way. Hang on. No need to take sides. You can cook, serve, eat and ENJOY natural foods without going near a health food store. I don't know whether your hair will be shinier, your skin clearer and your libido livelier. I do know that fresh fruits and vegetables and homemade bread are guaranteed to please young and old, health food nuts and gourmets.

A few generalities add up to a more natural way of cooking.

Make your own breads frequently and include flours such as unbleached, stone-ground whole wheat, rye, buckwheat and soy.

Serve whole grain cereals and sprinkle them with toasted wheat germ, nuts or raisins.

Serve brown rice and whole-grain pasta.

Sweeten fruits, cereals, puddings and custards with honey or pure maple syrup.

Summer Soup

Beat 4 *cups plain yogurt* until smooth. Add ½ *cup chopped walnuts,* 2 *cups peeled, diced cucumbers, salt* and *pepper,* and crushed *garlic* to taste. Mix and chill. Just before serving add an *ice cube* and a *walnut half* to each bowl. Serves 4.

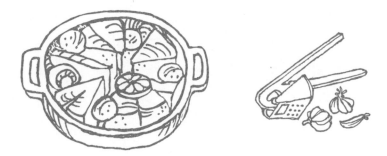

Sauteed Fish Filets

The most natural beginning for this recipe is a fishing expedition. But you can begin with frozen *fish filets.* Either way, coat the fish with *whole wheat flour* seasoned with *salt* and *pepper.* You know the neat way: put *flour* and *seasonings* in a paper bag, toss fish in and rattle around until fish is coated. Now saute fish in *sesame oil.* Serve with *lemon wedges.*

Steamed Spinach

Heat ¼ *cup sesame seed oil* or soy oil with a *clove of garlic,* mashed. Add 2 *pounds fresh spinach* — washed of course. Cover tightly and cook over very low heat about 7 minutes. Serves 4.

Cinnamon Raisin Muffins

Begin with a big earthenware bowl. Actually, you can use any sort of bowl, but natural baking is an affair of the spirit as well as a practicality, and there is something soul satisfying about an earthenware bowl and a wooden spoon. In the bowl, put 1 ½ *cups whole wheat flour,* ⅓ *cup brown sugar,* 3 *teaspoons baking pow-*

der, salt, 1 teaspoon cinnamon and *¾ cup unsulphured raisins.*
Mix this all around with your wooden spoon. Add *⅔ cup milk,*
⅓ cup soy oil and *2 eggs,* lightly beaten. Mix this around, but not
too much. Just to moisten everything. Fill greased muffin pans,
⅔ full. Bake in preheated 400° oven about 20 minutes. Makes 12.

Health food purists turn down dessert, but they'll eat this. So
will you. So will any and everyone in sight.

Honey Mousse

Separate *2 eggs.* Beat *1 egg* and *2 egg yolks* until light. With the
same beater, beat in *¾ cup honey* until light. Put in top part of
double boiler over hot water and cook, beating with a wire whisk
until thickened. Cool. Chill. With a *clean* beater, *beat the 2 egg*
whites until stiff. Whip *1 cup heavy cream* and fold it and the
egg whites into the yellow mixture. Put in shallow 1½ quart glass
dish. Cover and freeze several hours. Spoon into dishes, drizzle
with *honey.* (Technically, drizzle is a technical word, but I'm sure
you can figure it out. Basically, it means, don't drown the food
you're putting sauce on.) For a festive touch, which will please
your health food fans, too, sprinkle with chopped *pistachio nuts.*

THE ENTERTAINING BRIDE

There are a lot of good things about giving a party. You know who the guests are going to be. You can be sure of liking everything on the menu. And when the party's over, you don't have to go home.

If the thought of giving a party scares you, don't think about it. Do it. Begin by saying when. There are all sorts of interesting possibilities. Brunch. Lunch. Tea. Cocktails. Sit-down dinners. Buffets. Suppers. Invite your favorite people and dress yourself and your table to suit the occasion.

A word about party looks. You and your table should look pretty. But if you're doing the cooking, remember that flowing sleeves may flow into the soup tureen, trailing skirts may trip you up, if you wear a wool turtleneck sweater, you may roast along with the roast.

Say "party" and most people think "flowers." If your man does, lucky you. Happily, flowers aren't the only way to make a party table look exciting. Color counts for a lot. Plan a color scheme and carry it out with napkins and candles. For the ultimate in economy, buy the most beautiful fruits you can find, heap them high, and eat them afterward. Collect shells and driftwood for a seafood dinner. And make sure that everything shines. China. Silver. Glass. All that glitters may not be gold but it surely looks festive.

Guests invariably adjure you not to go to a lot of trouble. Pay no attention to them. Go to a lot of trouble. But go to it before your guests arrive. Then join them for a superb party. After all, you're not just giving this party, you're going to it, too, and you want to enjoy yourself. Fresh-squeezed orange juice, brewed coffee, Parmesan cheese grated from a big, fragrant chunk, are more trouble than their frozen, dried and cardboard contained counterparts. But they are part of the difference between a party and a meal. Does this mean you should slave over a hot stove all day? Not at all. It does mean you should avoid anything imitation, second-best, ordinary and boring.

BRUNCH

Restaurant menus usually list "fresh fruit in season." It's a lot more dramatic to serve fresh fruit *out* of season. Cantaloupe, for example, is nothing special in the summertime. In December, it's a refreshing surprise. Fresh berries, too, are downright dazzling in midwinter, especially if you garnish the serving bowl with a few shiny green leaves. Fresh fruits are more expensive out of season, so if you're economizing, you might prefer to derive your element of surprise by devising interesting combinations. Green grapes and canned purple plums. Apricots and raspberries. Fresh pineapple and frozen strawberries.

Drinks you'll leave to the man of the house. Bloody Marys are traditional and if you're having a crowd, some sparkly sort of punch. Coffee of course. Plan on having a lot and then double the amount. You needn't serve any appetizers or canapes. After all, food is coming. A bevy of imaginative breadstuffs and an interesting casserole. Here are some good ones.

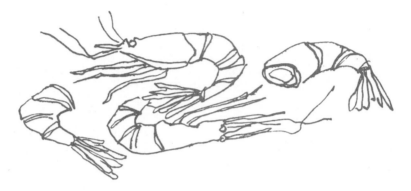

Shrimp Newburg Casserole

In a medium saucepan, combine *2 cans frozen condensed cream of shrimp soup* and *1 can evaporated milk* (13 oz.) Heat to boiling, stirring occasionally. Remove from heat. Add *1 cup shredded natural cheddar cheeze* (4 oz.), *2/3 cup mayonnaise;* stir till cheese melts. Blend *1/4 cup dry sherry.* Add *1 pound cleaned, cooked medium shrimp* and *4 cups cooked medium noodles.* Turn into 2 quart casserole. Bake in 350° oven 25 minutes, covered. Uncover; wreathe with *broken potato chips.* Return to oven; bake 5 minutes more. Serves 8 to 10.

Jambalaya

Chop up *2 onions* and toss them in a saucepan with *2 tablespoons of oil.* Heat to gild lightly. Add *2 pounds lean cubed pork.* When pleasantly brown, add *2 cups cubed ham.* Cook for a few minutes longer and then transfer it all to a good-sized casserole. Pour in *2 cups raw (uncooked) rice.* Pour on *8 cups boiling water.* Add *1 cup sherry, 1 teaspoon thyme* and a dash of *pepper.* Stir. Cover. Bake in a 325° oven for 40 minutes. Serves 8.

Mushamzu

Saute a few *chopped onions in butter*. Add as much sliced *zucchini squash* as you figure you'll need. (Are you feeding a few or a crowd?) Add as many *mushrooms* as your budget will allow. When just gently heated, not mushy, despite the name of this dish, spoon in 2 or if you're making a lot, 3 *cartons sour cream*. Keep hot but don't let it boil. Serve with grilled Canadian Bacon.

Of course, you don't have to have a casserole. Consider, instead, French toast, crepes or big, fat lumberjack pancakes with a choice of fruit compote or creamed chicken. Or brush spareribs with Worcestershire sauce, bake on a rack in a pan in a 400° oven. Pour off drippings and reduce heat to 350°. Brush with orange marmalade and bake 20 minutes more. 6 pounds of spareribs will serve 8 to 10 depending on what else you offer. Even scrambled eggs can be festive. Try these.

85

Swiss Scrambled Eggs

Empty 3ounce *jar dried beef* into a bowl and cover with boiling water. Let it stand for a minute, then drain. Put ¼ *cup* of that *bacon fat* you've been saving in a skillet. Or use butter or oil. Beat

12 *eggs* with ¾ *cup cream,* 1½ *teaspoons grated onion,* 1 *tea-spoon salt* and a dash of *pepper*. Pour into skillet. Cook over low heat, stir with fork, scraping cooked portions from pan until the eggs are almost set. Now add the beef along with ½ *pound Swiss cheese* cut into ¼ inch strips. Cook about 2 minutes more until the cheese begins to melt. Serves 10.

DESSERT LUNCHEONS

In the olden days, luncheons were for ladies who came in hats and gloves and ate creamed chicken in patty shells and desserts that weren't on their diet. Nowadays, ladies' luncheons occur more often in connection with a work session of some sort. Often the way it works is for everyone to bring her own sandwich, with coffee and dessert supplied by the hostess. When you're it, the party mood's best served by serving something a bit different. Apple pie and chocolate cake are fine fare, but since everyone knows what's in her sandwich, it's more fun to have dessert be more of a surprise. Here are some suggestions.

Crème de Menthe Sherbet Ring with Strawberries

Let 3 *pints lemon sherbet* soften in the refrigerator — about 30 minutes. Turn sherbet into a large bowl. Beat with portable electric mixer until smooth but not melted. Stir in 1 *jigger crème de menthe*. Turn mixture into a 5½ cup ring mold; freeze until firm — several hours or overnight. Meanwhile, wash *strawberries;* drain. Refrigerate until ready to use. To serve, invert ring mold over round, chilled serving platter. Place hot damp cloth over mold; shake to release sherbet. Fill center of ring with strawberries. Dust berries lightly with *sugar*. Serve at once. Makes 8 servings.

Eugenie Torte

Mix *2 cups sifted flour, 1 cup butter* (½ lb.) and *two 3-ounce packages soft cream cheese* until they are well blended. Wrap this dough in waxed paper and cool in refrigerator for 12 hours. Roll out paper-thin. You may need a tiny bit of extra *flour* to ease handling, but use as little as possible. Use a 9-inch pie or cake tin as if it were a big cookie cutter to cut out rounds. Bake these rounds of dough on an ungreased tin in a 425° oven for about 12 minutes. Watch carefully. This amount of dough makes about 8 wafer thin layers. Cool.

Whip *1 pint heavy cream* until stiff, adding just a touch of *sugar.* Then spread each pastry circle with *raspberry jam* — very, very carefully — and then with the whipped cream. Lay each pastry circle atop the other, until all have been covered with cream and jam. Cover entire cake with remaining cream and decorate with raspberry jam.

Brandied Apricots

Drain *canned apricots,* and save half the syrup. Combine syrup with an equal amount of *brandy.* Pour over apricots and refrigerate overnight.

Mandarin Orange Pie

Melt ¼ *pound butter* in a frying pan. Add *2 cups shredded coconut,* stir until golden brown. While warm, pat into pie pan. Set aside. Drain *2 small cans mandarin orange segments.* Save the liquid and boil it with enough water to make 1½ cups. Dissolve *1 package orange Jell-O™* in boiling liquid. Now add *1 pint vanilla ice cream,* a spoonful at a time, into the hot Jell-O. Set in refrigerator 45 minutes to set lightly. When cool, spoon into pie crust and return to refrigerator for 1 or 2 hours until firm. Before serving, spread with *whipped cream* and garnish with mandarins and coconut.

DIFFERENT LUNCHEONS

Now and again, however, you're going to want to give a lovely little luncheon where nobody brings anything. You're also not going to want to spend all day preparing it. Because, inevitably, dinner follows, and if you're married you're going to have to do something about that, too. Don't panic. There are all manner of luncheon menus that don't take hours of toiling, are serve-yourself, and can even be used-up at dinner or even the next day. Here are some suggestions:

Luncheon à la California

Halve ripe *avocados.* Leave the peel on. Fill with *chicken salad, tuna salad* or *egg salad* which you have made yourself or, if you're really in a hurry, purchased from the delicatessen. Garnish with *toasted walnuts.*

Serve an interesting bread. Sourdough, perhaps, and sweet butter. Tangerine sherbet and chocolate cookies for dessert.

Spring Luncheon

Cook lots of *fresh asparagus.* A good way is to scrub the stalks, tie them in a bunch, and stand the bunch upright in your coffee percolator. Cook five or ten minutes, uncovered, then cover and cook five minutes more. This way, the stalks will be tender-crisp and the heads intact, which heads ought always to be, n'est pas? Catch the string with a fork when you're lifting the asparagus out. This sounds like a lot of trouble, but we're talking about 17 minutes. Melt some *butter,* and toast some *bread.* Lay the asparagus on the toast and pour melted butter on top.

Serve with hard cooked eggs, iced tea — first of the season — and macaroons.

Italian Luncheon

Create a giant antipasto and let your guests make a meal of it. Begin with a bed of *watercress* or *endive.* Add pieces of *tuna, pickled beet cubes, olives, ripe* and *pimento-stuffed, hard-cooked egg slices, marinated artichoke hearts, pickled mushrooms,* cubes of *cooked ham,* small *green peppers.* Serve with bread sticks or hot garlic bread. Tortoni or spumoni for dessert.

It's-Cold-Outside-Luncheon

Good after skating or sledding or skiing or snowmobiling. Make *New England clam chowder* extra good and fast by adding extra canned *minced clams* to canned soup and using *heavy cream* as part of the liquid. Serve with pilot crackers, Winesap apples and gingersnaps.

DINNER PARTIES

Relax. Giving a dinner party isn't hard. In fact, it's often easier than other parties because you've had more practice. After all, you've been having little dinner-parties-for-two almost every night, haven't you? Well, just expand the menu, set a few more places, and go through your paces.

A few things to remember. Figure out what you'll need by way of serving dishes and have them on hand. If everything on your menu calls for a big, flat platter and you have only one, borrow some platters or change your menu. But do it before you take your roast from the oven.

Speaking of roasts, they are ideal for dinner parties. They more or less watch themselves — more, if you have a meat thermometer. And anything in a huge succulent hunk tends to look more hospitable than bits and pieces. Leg of lamb, roast of beef, roast pork, baked ham. They're all good. Conversely, broiled things — lamb chops, chicken, veal chops — are not my idea of a good time because you have to rush into the kitchen at the last minute — a minute before the punch line — or risk burning the whole business. If you have a lot of guests, you have to handle a lot of hot chops and plates and unless you're a circus juggler, that's hard.

With your roast, I'd serve an oven-baked vegetable. Candied sweet potatoes with ham, baked, creamed spinach with beef or lamb, oven-baked rice pilaf. Again, this saves pot-watching, and lets you spend more time with your guests.

If you serve hors d'oeuvres before dinner — and there's no need to — keep them simple. You want your guests to have room for the main course, and you want your stove and oven free to prepare it. A bowl of crisp raw vegetables and a shaker of seasoned salt is a nice prelude. If you want a real, honest-to-goodness first course, it's easiest to serve it in the living room while you're serving drinks. Hot or jellied consomme in cups. Melon and prosciutto. A tiny plate of antipasto for each guest. Some hostesses favor this practice because it writes a tactful finale to the drinking and gets guests into the dining room for dinner on time.

Sans help, the smoothest way to manage a sit-down dinner is to have the food on a buffet table, where guests can fill a plate and take it to the dinner table and sit down. If you have only a few guests, and your menu features individual servings — pot pies, cornish hens, filet mignons — you can have the food ready and waiting on heated plates.

Bread and a pot of sweet butter can be quite pretty on a table, but I'd keep bowls of vegetables and gravy off. After all, the boarding-house look is not what we're after. If you have a tea cart, draw it up beside the host or hostess and serve seconds, sauces and such from there.

Dessert and coffee can be served either at the table or back in the living room. Either way involves some clearing up. Glasses and hors d'oeuvre plates from the living room, dinner plates from the dining room. All I can say, is do it with as little fuss as possible. And try to prevent all of your women guests from leaping up to help. If you discover a way to do this, let me know. It ruins the conversation, creates chaos in the kitchen, makes the cook nervous and gets the drycleaner more business. But guests persist in insisting. You can only be as firm as possible and cherish the occasional guest who stays put and captivates one and all with tales of the African veldt until you get the parfaits compiled.

THE OUTDOOR BRIDE

I love drifting about a terrace or porch, wearing a long skirt, pouring something cold from a crystal pitcher, while rock cornish hens turn merrily on the barbecue spit and the stars come out overhead. I also love beachcombing all day in rolled-up dungarees, building a driftwood fire, and sipping beer and munching potato chips while a thick steak charcoal broils. The point is, these outdoor activities are poles apart. The former I call patio pyrotechnics. The latter: real-live-honest-to-goodness roughing it. As long as you don't mix them up, outdoor cooking's a breeze.

For the patio, porch, terrace, garden, roof or whatever al fresco arrangements your home has, feel free to peruse the colorful pages of your favorite house-and-garden type magazine. Candles in hurricane lamps? Why not? Potted geraniums? Fresh mushrooms in the tossed salad? Basting sauce compounded of melted currant jelly and sherry? Strawberries Romanoff for dessert? Yes, you may have them all. Just check the premises for insects. A bit of pre-guest spraying never hurts. Be sure you have enough light, but not too much. Build the fire well ahead of time and be patient. If it surely must be burned-down enough by now, it usually isn't. Supply big, big napkins if you're serving finger food. And don't forget to look up. That's where the stars are.

ROUGHING IT

For real live roughing it, forget all the menus you read for outdoor feasting and remember the number three. It's the secret of success. It means: plan to cook and eat three things. Period. Be sure they're absolutely superb things and have plenty. Add your favorite drink and have fun. Sing. Gather shells. Go wading.

You'll have time, and your dinner won't suffer because it's so simple. On the other hand, plan a menu even the tiniest bit more complex, and disasters begin to befall. It seems simple enough to toss a salad out of doors, and then a gale wind springs up, or it gets dark and you can't find the garlic clove much less the packet of dried herbs which were going to make it gourmet. When you're roughing it, you won't have a table, and until you try it, you can't imagine how confusing it is to locate things in high grass, a cardboard box, or the stern of a rowboat. So choose three and spree. I promise you, when the fresh air whips up appetites, and the food is delicious and plentiful, nobody will ask for variety. What can you do with three as the limiting factor? How about steak, buttered French bread, and candied apples on a stick? Or chicken, tomatoes and chocolate cake. Or shish kebab, Syrian bread and baklava. Buy the Syrian bread and baklava. There are lots of good recipes for shish kebab. Here is one:

Shish Kebab

In some markets, you can buy *lamb cubed* for shish kebab. If not, buy a leg of lamb, and have the butcher bone it for you. Cube the meat and put it in a bowl. Add *½ onion, thinly sliced, some salt, pepper* and *½ teaspoon oregano*. Refrigerate as long as you

like but at least 1 hour. Alternate meat cubes, *pineapple chunks, onion pieces* and *cherry tomatoes* on metal skewers. Roll in vegetable oil. Broil over charcoal or wood fire.

93

Outdoor Coffee

Of course, you know how to make coffee. But outdoors, your way may be complicated. Drip coffee requires a kettle and a pot.

Perk coffee may refuse to perk for practically forever. Even instant coffee can be hard to manage if you're trying to put ten teaspoons of powder into ten cups with a high wind blowing. It's easier to do this: Put *½ cup instant coffee* in a large enameled coffeepot or kettle. Add *2 quarts cold water*. Stir to combine. Cover pot. Place on grill, 3 inches above prepared coals. Let coffee come to a boil. It takes about 20 minutes. Remove to edge of grill and let stand about 5 minutes to steep.

Dessert on the Grill

You'll need: *graham crackers, marshmallows* and *chocolate bars*. Toast the marshmallows — two at a time — over the hot coals. Remove from stick and immediately put a marshmallow on a cracker, top with chocolate, put another marshmallow on top of that, cover with another cracker. Squeeze together to melt the chocolate and form the gooiest, goodiest, messiest morsel imaginable.

Bananas on the Grill

You'll need: *bananas, brown sugar* and *sour cream*. Put unpeeled bananas at edge of grill over prepared coals. Grill, turning occasionally, until banana skins burst and juices bubble. Using tongs, remove to serving dishes. Peel. Top with sour cream and brown sugar.

PATIO PLEASURES

As we were saying, when you're doing your outdoor cooking close to home, anything goes and the more courses the merrier. You can even prepare some dishes ahead of time. In fact, it's a very good idea to. You can then concentrate on some plain and fancy grillwork without trying to be indoors and out all at once. Some good go-withs include casseroles of all kinds. A good kind is:

Three-Bean Casserole

In a small skillet, saute in butter some chopped onion and garlic. Toss this into a 2-quart casserole. Add *2 cans kidney beans, 1 can green beans*, drained, and *1 can beans with tomato sauce*. Add *1 tablespoon brown sugar, 1 teaspoon dry mustard, ½ cup catsup, 1 tablespoon vinegar* and a dash of *salt* and *pepper*. Bake covered

in 350° oven for 35 minutes. Ten minutes before you're ready to serve, take the cover off and bake till serving time. Do give it a stir now and again.

Super Scalloped Potatoes

95

Prepare *one or more packages of scalloped potatoes* as package label directs. Bake until golden brown. Spread *whipped cream* over hot potatoes and sprinkle with *shredded Swiss cheese*. Run under the broiler until top is golden.

Tomato Scallop

Put 2 or more *cans Italian tomatoes,* drained, into a greased baking dish. Top with plenty of soft *white bread crumbs,* sprinkled with *sugar, salt, oregano* and *rosemary.* Drizzle with *melted butter.* Bake uncovered in 350° oven about 45 minutes.

We said you'd have time for fancy grillwork if you did your casserole work ahead of time. So here's how.

Barbecued Plant Chops

Basic ingredients here are *lamb chops* and *egg plant.* You can use shoulder chops because marinating things tends to tenderize them and we're about to marinate. Combine: ½ *cup salad oil,* ¼ *cup olive oil,* ½ *cup lemon juice,* 2 *tablespoons oregano,* 1 *teaspoon salt* and ½ *cup white wine.* Put chops in a large baking dish. Peel the eggplant and cut it crosswise into half-inch thick slices. Put them in the baking dish, too. Pour marinade over all. Refrigerate at least two hours. Grill chops and eggplant slices ten minutes on each side. To serve: place eggplant slice on top of chop and if you're feeling fancy, a slice of *lemon* on top of that.

Serve with rice and fresh apricots for dessert.

Rumakibobs

Wrap *chicken livers* (raw) in *bacon* (raw) and thread on skewers alternately with *mushroom caps* and *pineapple chunks.* Broil 3 minutes. Turn and broil 4 minutes longer.

Grapeach Pie

Bake a frozen *pie shell* and let it cool. Put 7 or 8 peeled, halved *peaches,* cut side down, in the pie shell. Arrange 1 *cup seedless green grapes* in and around the peaches. Make a pretty glaze: Sprinkle 1½ *teaspoons unflavored gelatin* over 2 *tablespoons cold water.* Let stand to soften. In a small saucepan heat 1 *cup peach jam.* Remove from heat. Add gelatin mixture, stirring to dissolve. Stir in ¼ *cup Madeira wine.* Pour glaze over fruit. Refrigerate about 2 hours. Serve with *whipped cream.*

ICE CREAM IDEAS

Della Robia

Wash, dry, sugar and chill all the pretty fresh fruit you can afford: raspberries, strawberries, blueberries, peaches, honeydew melon balls, cherries. Find a big, big platter. On it heap coffee ice cream. Wreath the ice cream with the fruit. Serve with whipped cream laced with rum.

Black Cherries Aflame

Drain 1 *can black cherries.* Save the juice. Pour 2 *jiggers Cointreau* over the cherries and let stand. Just before serving, add 4 *jiggers cherry juice* and heat. Add 2 *jiggers brandy.* Put a match to it and serve flaming over 1 *quart vanilla ice cream.* Serves four.

Lemon Parfait   97

Mix 1 *cup whipped cream* with 1 *pint lemon ice cream.* Put it into 4 parfait glasses. Make a hole down the center and fill each with 1 *jigger Curaçao.* Top with whipped cream and shavings of *bitter chocolate.*

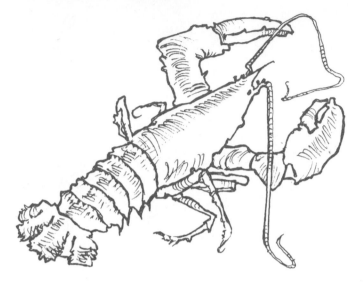

SWOON FOOD

Disregard the latest scientific information. Food is an aphro-
disiac. I don't mean dried bat's wings or the skin of a snake shed
by the light of a sickle moon. I don't even mean gensing root. I do
mean swoon food. Which is exactly what the name implies. Food
worth swooning over. Note the word "worth". We are not talking
here about super personal yummies. If you're crazy about pickle-
peanut butter sandwiches with onion, eat them when he's at the
office. Even if your idea of a top taste titillation is to munch your
way through a whole box of Mallomars, do it when you're alone.
Sensuous eating, like a lot of other lovely things, takes two. So
plan something that you, he, and anyone else in his right mind,
will swoon over.

98   The ultimate point and purpose of course is to have him swoon
over you. So it's important not to plan something that involves
reddening your eyes chopping onions, or ruining your hairdo over
a steaming pot of noodles. I know Sophia Loren can look ravishing
when she's up to her elbows in pasta, but unless you're an Italian
movie star, I don't advise you to try it.

Shrimp Velvet

What I would advise is to snip, with your trusty scissors, a few lengths of *fresh chives* into a saucepan with *2 tablespoons of butter*. Add *1½ pounds raw shrimp,* shelled and deveined, a pinch of *thyme,* a *bay leaf* and a scattering of *salt* and *pepper*. Simmer 7 or 8 minutes. Warm *2 tablespoons brandy,* pour over the shrimp, light. When the flame dies, add *¾ cup white wine*. Simmer 3 minutes. Transfer shrimp to a warm dish. Mix together *1 cup cream, 2 egg yolks, 1 teaspoon lemon juice* and *1 teaspoon chopped parsley, chervil* and *tarragon*. Add to saucepan. Stir. Do not let boil. Pour over the shrimp.

Serve with Minute Rice, green salad, and the rest of the wine.

Don't forget to light the candles. And if you usually wear your hair up, let it down. If you usually wear it down, put it up. Variety is the spice of wife.

If you have a fireplace, curl up before it, play your favorite records, while some very elegant veal chops bake-without-watching in the oven. You choose the music, I'll tell you how to make the chops. Like this.

Veal Chops

Brown some very nice *veal chops* in *butter*. Place them in a baking dish. Mix some *bread crumbs, Parmesan cheese, minced par*

sley, salt and *pepper* and enough *white wine* to make a paste. Spread this on the chops, dot with *butter* and bake uncovered in a 300° oven 45 minutes. When he changes the records, you can baste the chops with *consomme,* but you don't have to, until the end. Now, drop a spoonful of *sour cream* on each chop and serve. With tiny peas and icy marinated artichoke hearts.

And more is more so. If you're crazy about *caviar,* and can't afford to serve it at your own parties, why not make a meal of it. A big bountiful bowl of caviar, with the traditional trimmings — chopped, hard-cooked egg, lemon slices, melba toast. Nothing else. Except champagne, of course.

If *fresh asparagus* is your his-and-her thing, celebrate spring with great green heaps of asparagus, cooked just the merest three minutes, served with butter. Sugar cookies and coffee for dessert.

Mushrooms are another food it feels lovely to have more of. Buy big white *mushrooms,* saute them in *butter* — not margarine, this time — and at the last, stir in *1 cup sour cream.* Serve with chunks of French bread to sop up the sauce with.

100

What's un-sensuous? Anything he hates. Anything you hate. Raw onions. Spare ribs. Hamburgers. Tripe unless he's French. Squid unless he's Italian or Greek. Lobster unless somebody else cooks and serves it; if they do, it's very, very sensuous. Dry cereal.

There are some fine distinctions. Milk is not sensuous, heavy cream is. Espresso is sensuous, a mug of instant coffee is not. Baked potato with sour cream and bacon is, French fries are not. Sandwiches are not, hot rolls are. Getting down to generalities, smooth is, lumpy is not; rich is, heavy is not; piquant is, spicy is not; largesse is, surfeit is not. How do you know? Ask this question about the menu you have in mind: would it be good for serving in bed on a silver tray with a long-stemmed red rose in a crystal vase? If so, serve it any way you please. If not, reach for the silver tray. Un-sensuous menus need all the help they can get.

EATING IN BED

Wives spend a lot of time devising tempting tray meals for invalid husbands who are usually so angry at being sick that they

don't notice what they're eating except to complain about it. The thing to do when your husband has the 'flu is give him what the doctor ordered and go read War and Peace. Then when nobody's sick and there's no reason to eat in bed except for the fun of it, concoct some all-out opulent in-bed eating. No mundane crackers-and-milk snack, but a bountiful bedded board. It's not hard, but there are a few tricks to it. The cardinal rule is to have everything ready at the same time or you'll defeat your whole purpose and be jumping in and out of bed disarranging the blankets and blancmange. You'll be creating a transportation problem if you plan a meal with too many components. 12-boy curry is not for bed. Get out your largest tray and plan accordingly. It's hard to cut in bed which gives lobster newburg an edge over rack of lamb. Avoid finger foods like chicken in a basket unless you like sleeping on greasy percale. Which leaves roughly a thousand and one nights of delights.

Stew, you know how to make that. The recipe's on page 28.

Chile con Carne. Buy it at the local chili parlor or heat up a few cans. Serve with corn chips and beer.

Lobster Newburg

Comes frozen or canned. Or make your own Newburg Sauce this way. Melt *2 tablespoons butter,* add *¼ cup sherry* or Madeira wine. Cook 2 minutes. Add *1 cup cream.* Pour a few spoonsful over 3 well beaten *egg yolks.* Mix thoroughly then stir eggs into rest of sauce. Let cook until it thickens, stirring constantly. Add *2 cups lobster* or *shrimp,* and stir until warmed thoroughly. Serve over rice.

Giant Hamburgers

with Roquefort Cheese melted on top. Serve with thick icy-cold slices of tomato and glasses of milk.

THE DISAPPEARING BRIDE

DO IT WITH DIET

Don't worry, it happens to the best of brides. You wake up one day, try on last year's bikini and decide that some of you has got to go. Say five or six pounds of you. When you were single the next step was obvious. Fill the refrigerator with celery and cottage cheese and stop cooking. Now the problem is more complex. What you're trying to do now is lose pounds without losing the pleasure of your husband's company at the dinner table.

If you're not serving dinner, you can't very well expect him to rush home to it. You can, of course, cook fabulous, fattening feasts, and serve them to him while you nibble on a lettuce leaf. You can if you have the will power. I don't. And none of my friends do. But we may be a flabby-willed bunch. But even if you manage it, it's bound to make your man feel guilty. Nor, in my opinion, does pleasant dinner conversation consist of exclamations: "Is that all you're eating? Ugh."

How then do you disappear before your husband's eyes? One workable way is to limit your cuisine to low calorie vegetables and broiled lean meats. Since broiled lean meats can include steak, chops and chicken, most men won't mind. For a while. But when he starts reminiscing about the fried chicken in cream gravy his mother used to make, or worse still, when he starts talking about the Beef Stroganoff his old girl friend used to serve, it's time to get creative about your low calorie cooking.

I don't go along with the idea that you can de-calorize anything and everything. Sweetening rhubarb with a sugar substitute saves a million calories and tastes fine. But a hot fudge sundae made with ice milk, diet sauce and low calorie whip topping is not a hot fudge sundae, it's a travesty. Ditto for strawberry short-

cake sans shortcake and clotted cream. Also, many low-calorie foods on your supermarket shelf are a snare and a delusion. They're not that low in calories, they don't taste that good, and they do cost more.

The answer is to serve regular food in interesting ways that don't up the calorie count. Recipes follow. But first some helpful generalities.

Make mealtime an event. Eat slowly. Don't eat while you're watching TV. You needn't eat a lot to feel satisfied if you've been feasting your eyes on a pretty centerpiece, glittering glassware, candles and such.

Outwit your appetite with a bowl of hot consomme before your meal. Vary this with hot tomato juice or clear turtle soup for an occasion. Hot liquids are generally more satisfying than cold, but in summer, try icy clam cocktail or sauerkraut juice.

Fish, chicken and veal are the leanest of meats. Serve them often. Trim visible fat off beef and lamb.

Skip bread and dessert.

At snacktime, nibble raw carrots, sour pickles, fresh mushrooms, celery, bean sprouts.

Lean hard on herbs and spices for flavor. They won't add calories. But don't use large amounts of catsup or chili sauce. Both contain a good deal of sugar. Worcestershire sauce, soy sauce and lemon juice, on the other hand, are your allies. Cooking with wine is fine, too, because most of the alcohol evaporates in the cooking.

Veal Ragout

Brown *2½ pounds very lean veal cubes*. If you're being fierce about eliminating fat, use a Teflon-lined pan. Otherwise, a tiny bit of vegetable oil will be fine. Remove veal to a casserole, and in the same skillet, heat *2 sliced onions* until they wilt. Put these in the casserole. Drain *two 1-ounce cans of mushrooms* and put the liquid into the casserole along with *2 cups white wine, 1 teaspoon rosemary* and a bit of *garlic salt*. Cover and bake in 350° oven for an hour. Add mushrooms and continue cooking until they're heated and you're ready to serve. Nice with green salad. And, if you can bear it, hot rolls for him.

Lamb Steak Crème de Menthe

Sprinkle *lamb steaks* with *garlic salt* and *pepper*. Saute in a non-stick skillet, turning several times. Ten minutes should do it. Remove steaks and pour in *crème de menthe — ¼ cup or so —* and *1 teaspoon Worcestershire sauce* and a little water. Heat until bubbly and pour over lamb. If you have fresh mint growing, throw a few leaves into the sauce and use a few more for garnish.

Foo Yong

Beat *six eggs* and add any or all of the following: chopped *bamboo shoots*, chopped *water chestnuts*, shredded *Chinese pea pods*, *bean sprouts*, *chopped shrimp*. Saute in vegetable oil about five minutes.

Slim-style Ratatouille

The traditional Provençal version of this dish is redolent with olive oil. Leaving the oil out does change the taste but it also does nice things for your waist. It still tastes good — just different.

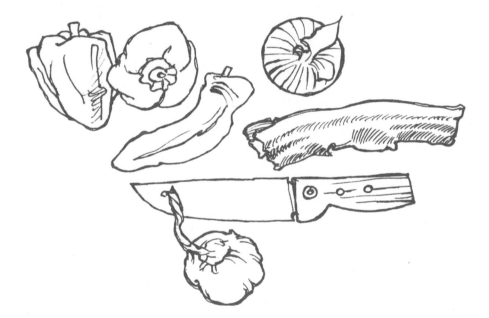

Cook an *eggplant* (peeled and cubed) and five or six sliced *zucchini* in boiling salted water for about five minutes. You're making a lot because it keeps well and is nice for company. Remove and drain and put in a large, shallow baking dish. Sprinkle with chopped *fresh parsley, salt, garlic salt, 2 teaspoons oregano* and *2 cans Italian-style tomatoes*. Bake for half an hour. Serve to 8. Or save to reheat. You can even serve it cold.

Filet of Sole with grapes

Sprinkle *sole* with *salt* and *pepper* and place in greased, shallow baking dish. Top sole with *fresh mushroom caps* and *seedless white grapes*. Pour *1 cup dry white wine* in, cover, and bake at 350°, covered, for half an hour.

Mushrooms Naturelle

Wipe *mushrooms* with a damp cloth. Put them in a shallow baking dish and sprinkle them with *salt, pepper,* chopped *fresh parsley* and chopped *fresh chives*. Cover very tightly with foil. Bake in a slow oven, 325°, for 15 minutes. When you take off the foil, there'll be juice, from the mushrooms themselves. Once you get used to the taste, you may like it better than the usual butter sauce. When you can't get fresh chives and parsley, you can use dried thyme and marjoram but the greenery is better.

DESSERT OR MUST YOU?

The best thing to do about dessert is skip it altogether. The second best thing to do is to choose cheese or fresh — not canned — fruit. However, there comes a time when none of this will do. What you want is a real live honest-to-goodness dessert dessert. Without abandoning your disappearing act, there are three things you can do.

1. Take a tiny, tiny taste of whatever it is you're perishing for. Fudge cake, Nesselrode pie, peach Melba. The easiest way to do this is to go to a restaurant, induce your husband to order the dessert you want, and snitch a taste.

2. Eat one (1) uno, a single, sole, solitary piece of angel food cake, sponge cake, chiffon cake. Only a hundred calories or so if you don't take seconds. Or one scoop of vanilla ice cream. Even one scoop of pistachio won't undo all if you stop with one.

3. Angel food cake is at least dependable. You may, of course, like some of the low calorie desserts that I don't. Most are made with sugar substitutes. Before you try to make up your own recipes, you should know that these substitutes stand in for sugar only insofar as sweetening is concerned. In cakes, for example, sugar supplies texture and bulk. There *is* one whole genre of desserts you can have fun with without adding bulk to your own. Fruits and such flambé. Here are some suggestions.

Peerless Pears

Simmer peeled fresh *pears* in water, *sugar substitute* and *1 teaspoon vanilla*. Ignite warmed *Kirsch* and pour over.

Pêche Flambé

Put some *peaches* — 3 or 4 if you're serving two, 5 or 6 if you're serving four — in a saucepan with some *water, lemon juice* and *sugar substitute*. Simmer, turning the fruit every few minutes. Remove, pour into heatproof baking dish or platter. Heat *light rum* and pour over, flaming.

At this point, you had better stop doing diet things. You don't want to disappear altogether. I shall refrain from reminding you that at no point are you likely to be able to stop cooking. The thought has inevitably occurred to you. I hope the thought has also occurred to you that being the power behind the menu is heady freedom. You can make your creamed chicken with real cream, leave the onions out of the ragout if you're not feeling oniony, put more nuts than flour in your nut bread and be absolutely certain of getting your lamb chops rare, medium or medium rare as the inclination strikes you.

THERE'S A MAN IN MY KITCHEN

My grandfather said that all of the world's great chefs were men. My grandfather was one of the world's great chefs. I learned half of what I know about cooking from him. I learned the other half from a man I considered marrying but decided not to because he cooked too well. He would stir my stew, season my ragout, turn the front burner down, the oven up and ultimately me off. Now that I'm older and wiser, I realize that we probably could have worked things out. I could have let him cook for a whole week without so much as a suggestion from me. The next week we could have reversed roles. I commend the idea if you happen to be married to a good cook. But you're probably not or you wouldn't be reading this book.

On the other hand. You are likely, more often than not, to have a man in your kitchen. Somehow the sights and sounds and smells of food preparation draw men like a magnet. In fact, if your husband is somewhere in the house and you don't want to call him, try rattling a spoon around in a mixing bowl.

If he's not cooking, a man in the kitchen tends to sit on counters, lift pot lids and nibble the back of your neck. I'd be inclined to encourage the sitting, tolerate the lifting, and drop everything in favor of giving total, undivided attention to the neck nibbling. There are few things more delightful than a perfectly cooked dinner. But there are some.

110

THE LAST WORD

Here we are at the end of a book to, for and about brides. And we've scarcely mentioned one word. Purposely. Because it's mentioned so often the eyes slide over it on the page. Yet it's the most important word in any book. Especially a book about cooking. Cook with it and your cooking will be beautiful. Live it and life will be good. The word is LOVE.

HOW MUCH TO BUY OF WHAT

Buying Fresh Vegetables for Two

Asparagus .... 1 pound
Beets .... 1 pound or 1 bunch

Carrots .... 1 bunch
Cauliflower .... ½ small head
Celery ....1 bunch
Corn on the cob .... 4 to 6 ears
Green beans .... ¾ pound
Lettuce .... 1 head
Onions .... ¼ pound

Peas .... 1 pound
Potatoes, sweet or white .... 1 pound
Spinach, swiss chard, beet or turnip greens .... ½ pound
Squash, winter or summer .... 1 or 1 pound

112

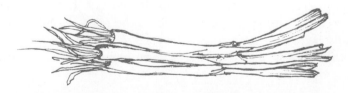

Apples .... Buy 3 to 5 pounds
    For eating, choose: Delicious, McIntosh, Northern Spy,
    Winesap.
    For pies and applesauce, choose: Grimes Golden, Jonathan,
    McIntosh, Northern Spy, Baldwin.
    For baking, choose: Northern Spy, Rome Beauty, Winesap.

Avocados .... 1 serves 2
Cherries .... ½ pound sweet serves 2
Melons: honeydew, cantaloupe or muskmelon .... 1 serves 2
Oranges .... Buy 6
Pineapples .... 1 serves 4 or 5

113

Buying Fish for Two

Fillets	¾ pound
Steaks	1 pound
Whole	1½ to 2 pounds
Lobster tails	6 to 8 ounce tail per serving
Oysters	1 pint
Shrimp	1 pound fresh or frozen

Buying Poultry for Two

Chicken for frying	1½ pound
Chicken for roasting	2½ to 3½ pound
Turkey	4 to 6 pounds

Buying Meat for Two

Beef

Pot roast	2 pounds
Oven roast	3 pound or 1 rib

Steak .... ½ to ¾ pound per serving
Liver .... ½ pound
Ground Beef .... ½ pound

Veal

Veal cutlets .... 1 pound
Veal roast .... 3 pounds

Lamb

Lamb chops .... 4 large, 6 small
Roast lamb .... 2½ pounds

Pork

Pork chops 4
Pork roast .... 3 to 4 pounds
Spareribs .... 2 pounds
Ham .... ½″ slice (1 pound)
Frankfurters .... 4 to 6

HOW TO STOCK YOUR PANTRY

Have-to-haves

Flour
Sugar, white and brown
Shortening
Vinegar
Oil
Baking powder
Baking soda
Coffee
Tea
Cake and biscuit mixes
Cereals, ready-to-eat and hot

Macaroni, spaghetti, noodles
Salt
Pepper
Cinnamon
Celery, onion and garlic salts
Parsley flakes
Chives, dried or dehydrated
Bouillon cubes
Worcestershire sauce
Vanilla

Nice-to-adds

Canned soups — especially
cream of mushroom
Lemon or lemon juice
Mustard

Catsup
Instant rice
Thyme, rosemary, dill,
marjoram, oregano, bay leaves

Perishable but pretty indispensable

Butter or margarine
Bread
Bacon

Eggs
Cheeses
Milk

Festive frills

Canned crab meat
Hollandaise sauce mix
Canned shrimp
Dried mushrooms
Wine — sherry, Burgundy,
dry white

Slivered almonds
Tuna
Canned artichoke hearts
Canned Newburg sauce
Brown gravy mix or
canned brown gravy

Index

119

121